XX

0924

£2

DEALING IN TRADED OPTIONS

DEALING IN TRADED OPTIONS

RICHARD HEXTON

The London School of Investment

PRENTICE HALL

NEW YORK   LONDON   TORONTO   SYDNEY   TOKYO

First published 1989 by
Prentice Hall International (UK) Ltd,
66 Wood Lane End, Hemel Hempstead,
Hertfordshire, HP2 4RG
A division of
Simon & Schuster International Group

Printed and bound in Great Britain at the University Press, Cambridge.

Library of Congress Cataloging-in-Publication Data

Hexton, Richard, 1948–
　　Dealing in traded options/Richard Hexton.
　　　p.　cm.
　　Includes index.
　　ISBN 0-13-198557-4
　　1. Options (Finance)　I. Title.
HG6024.A3H48　1988
332.64′52 – dc19　88-19507

British Library Cataloguing in Publication Data

Hexton, Richard, *1948–*
　　Dealing in traded options.
　　1. Stock markets. Traded options
　　I. title
　　332.64′52

　　ISBN 0-13-198557-4

1　2　3　4　5　92　91　90　89　88

0-13-198557-4

To my parents
Eileen and Leonard Hexton

CONTENTS

FOREWORD

Options trading can be traced back several hundred years but, it was not until 1973 that the World's first traded options market was formed in the United States. Since then traded options markets have been opened in most of the world's financial centres.

Traded options growth has, particularly in the last few years, been spectacular. In the UK the London Traded Options Market (LTOM) traded almost 12 million contracts in 1987, a greater volume in one year then the total number of contracts traded since the market was formed in 1978.

As the market has matured it has become more sophisticated and for the private client, in particular, it is essential that he fully appreciates the factors that can determine whether he makes a profit or a loss on each of the transactions he enters into. The information contained in this book should enable him to gain this appreciation and will appeal to both technical and fundamental analysts. While there is a significant section devoted to chartism it is well backed up by a fundamental examination of how an options premium can be affected by changes in underlying share price, volatility and time to expiration. Sections on the Black Scholes option pricing formula, the use of computers in technical analysis and a 'broker's view' give a good balance between theory and practice.

The UK investor has not been well served with books that specifically address his own market and this publication is therefore very welcome.

A. P. DE GUINGAND
Director
LONDON TRADED OPTIONS MARKET
THE INTERNATIONAL STOCK EXCHANGE

PREFACE

This book is aimed mainly at the private investor, but will also provide a useful reference guide for the professional. One of its aims is to present the subject in a clear and jargon-free style; another has been to ensure that the reader fully understands both the potential and the limitations of dealing in traded options before entering this market.

Properly managed, traded options are an investor's dream: they require minimal outlay, allow relatively easy management of risk, and can generate huge profits – irrespective of market trends. This book not only covers the basic elements of traded options for the novice; but also the more advanced valuation methods. It helps to illustrate how traded options may be used both for speculation and protection and discusses the flexibility and wide range of opportunities awaiting the potential investor.

One of the most important and unique features of this book is its logical progression of charting techniques and comprehensive use of technical analysis to show the importance of timing in making profits from traded options.

The traded options market is not a mystery and as you work your way through the book you will soon find yourself not only enjoying the concepts that traded options can offer; but hopefully benefiting from their rewards.

A word or two of advice: it is important to take just a few steps at a time; perhaps at first just get your feet wet with a few contracts. Then, once you feel more confident and have locked in some profits, consider diving from the high board.

Good luck with your dealing!

RICHARD HEXTON

ONE

AN INTRODUCTION TO TRADED OPTIONS

HISTORY OF THE TRADED OPTIONS MARKET

The concept of options can be traced back as far as the Middle Ages when they were used in their most basic form in the course of trade and commerce. Unfortunately, as the use of options became more widespread, so proper controls and safeguards became less effective.

In the seventeenth century the speculative use of options in the tulip industry in Holland had catastrophic results and eventually led to the virtual collapse of the Dutch economy. These and similar events did nothing to improve the reputation of the options market.

In this century the tax authorities were not slow to indicate their mistrust when, in the 1960s, many tax avoidance schemes were constructed using options as a screen. However, the Inland Revenue has now recognised the important role played by the options market and capital gains on traded options are taxed in the same way as any other security.

In 1973 the Chicago Board Options Exchange opened in America. In April 1978, Amsterdam negotiated with London to set up a joint European traded options market, and in the same year the London Traded Options Market (LTOM) was set up. Initially, there were a number of internal problems and the new London market was treated with some caution. The speculative nature of option trading and a lack of information made private investors reluctant to enter the market. However, by 1980 the atmosphere had changed considerably, the new market was firmly established and the increased public awareness brought about by privatisation had improved the general level of understanding.

'The London Traded Options Market of The International Stock Exchange' confirmed its little appreciated position as one of the world's fastest-growing markets when the twenty millionth options contract was traded on the market floor on 24 September 1987. The LTOM took from April 1978 until December

TABLE 1.1 Annual volume figures since 1978.

Year	Volume	Percentage increase	Accumulated volumes	Percentage increase
1978	107,564	—	107,564	—
1979	221,563	105.98	329,127	105.98
1980	253,481	14.41	582,608	77.02
1981	331,489	30.77	914,097	56.90
1982	479,805	44.74	1,393,902	52.49
1983	622,697	29.78	2,016,599	44.67
1984	1,120,573	79.95	3,137,172	55.57
1985	2,278,189	103.31	5,415,361	72.62
1986	5,360,127	135.28	10,775,488	98.98
1987*	12,242,190	128.39	23,017,678	113.61

* Annualised figures based on the nine months to September 1987.

1986 to trade its first ten million contracts and only took a further nine months to trade the next ten million option contracts.

Following a good, but unspectacular, growth period (at least as far as other options exchanges were concerned) from the market's inception in April 1978, interest in options on equities, gilts, currencies and the FT-SE 100 Index literally exploded in 1985. This enormous turnaround in the fortunes of the LTOM coincided with the formation of a practitioner led Options Committee and the highly professional approach to developing the business displayed by the management of the newly created Options Development Group. The dramatic impact of this new management structure can easily be illustrated by scanning annual volume figures for the market since 1978. (See Table 1.1.)

It can be readily seen how the innovations of 1985 have catapulted the LTOM into the position of the world's largest derivative products market outside the United States of America, and arguably made it the most dynamic and vigorous market in the world.

GROWTH OF THE MARKET

The traded options market has now reached a significant size. The average daily number of contracts is currently around 50,000 and over one million contracts are open, representing an underlying value well in excess of £4,000 million. Premiums paid have doubled since 1986 and are almost £3,000 million per annum. The market is liquid in active options, easily handling orders of 1,000 contracts.

The growth of the market exceeds 11 per cent per month compound. The figures in Table 1.2 illustrate the dynamism of the LTOM. During the first ten months of 1987 there will have been as many contracts as during the eight-year period since the inception of the market to the end of 1986.

TABLE 1.2 Annual totals of contracts traded.

Year	Total
1978	107,564
1979	221,563
1980	253,481
1981	331,489
1982	479,805
1983	622,697
1984	1,120,573
1985	2,278,189
1986	5,360,127
Up to 30.9.87	9,425,769

However, options on individual UK equities account for virtually all the growth that has occurred in the past two years. The volume of business in the FT-SE 100 Index option alone could, based on US experience, be as great as that in equity options, that is, a twenty-fold increase over current levels of business.

Given the size of the security business transacted within the Exchange and the related currency dealings, the traded options market can become the largest marked for derivative products in its time zone. It is possible that, within three to five years, the volume could grow to anywhere between 150,000 and one million contracts per day, with substantially higher peaks. Currently, there are options available on 62 shares, FT-SE Index, three-gilts convertible loan, and currency options on the dollar/sterling and dollar/Deutschmark exchange rates.

The LTOM has been created by the Stock Exchange so that investors can buy or sell 'options' in shares, without necessarily having to buy or sell the shares themselves. This facility allows enormous flexibility for investors both to protect themselves against risk and to seek speculative gains.

SELECTION OF STOCKS

In choosing the stocks on which traded options are to be listed, the Council of The Stock Exchange has regard to the needs and interests of all users of the market. It is essential for the integrity and well-being of the traded options market that there should be a free and liquid market in the underlying securities. The following are criteria employed in assessing the suitability of stocks for option trading:

1. The company's shares must be listed on The Stock Exchange.
2. During the five years prior to the introduction of option trading, the company must not have defaulted on the payment of any interest, dividend, or sinking fund instalment, or committed any breach of the provisions of any borrowing

limitation, of any loan stock, or of the Articles of Association which in the opinion of The Stock Exchange would render the company unsuitable for option trading.

3. The company must have a substantial equity market capitalisation and there should normally have been a free and active market in the shares for at least two years previously.
4. The company should normally have at least 10,000 equity shareholders.

WHAT ARE OPTIONS AND TRADED OPTIONS?

Many investors will be aware that there are conventional or traditional options and traded options. A traditional option can be taken out on any share (provided you can find a buyer) and is for a fixed period (usually three months). *Traded options are only available on certain shares nominated by The Stock Exchange.* As you progress through the book, you will learn the rules that govern dealings in traded options and how they differ from the traditional option contracts.

An option is a contract which confers the right (but not the obligation) to buy or sell as asset at a given price on (or before) a given date. Traded options are negotiable securities in their own right, and so can be bought or sold in the market. There are two types of options:

1. Call options. These give the holder the right to *buy* shares at a specified price – the 'exercise' price.
2. Put options. These give the holder the right to *sell* shares at a specified price – the 'exercise' price.

It is these options that can themselves be bought or sold at any time during their lifespan, independently of the underlying share to which they relate, that form the traded options market. The unique features are the following:

1. An option may be abandoned at any time.
2. The buyer's potential loss is limited to the price (premium) he paid for the option.

All call options on a particular underlying security are called a 'class'. Put options on the same security form a separate class.

Contracts

In traded options, the minimum trading unit is referred to as one 'contract'. A contract normally represents 1,000 shares in the underlying security. Thus, the purchase of one call option contract gives the buyer the right (or the option) to purchase 1,000 shares in the underlying security. These contracts are not divisible: in other words dealings are not allowed in fractions of a contract.

Contracts on some shares may be of a different size, particularly in shares of foreign companies whose unit share prices tend to be much higher than for UK domestic companies. Also, after capital changes within a company, there may have to be adjustments in the size of the contract to allow for, say, scrip issues or share splits.

See Appendix 3 for examples of contract notes.

Option lifespans

A traded option has a maximum lifespan of nine months which is determined by its 'expiry date'. Expiry dates are fixed at three-monthly intervals.

When a new company is introduced to the traded options market, it is allocated to one of three possible cycles of expiry dates:

(a) January, April, July, October;
(b) February, May, August, November;
(c) March, June, September, December.

There will always be three different expiry dates quoted in each class of option. In the first example, when the January expiry date is reached a new series of October options will be introduced, and when the April options expire the following January options will be introduced, and so on. The precise date in the month when options expire is published in the financial daily press and is also stated on the contract note.

'Rule 316' of The Stock Exchange sets out the normal expiry date of traded options and can be summarised as follows:

> To find the expiry date of a traded option series, look for the latest date within the expiry month, which is also the last day of dealings for a Stock Exchange account. The month's option series will normally expire two days prior to that date. If, for example, 26 October is the final day of dealings for that account, it will follow that the expiry date of that October series will be 24 October.

As already stated, the date on which an option's life comes to an end is known as the expiry date. It is the last day that the option can be exercised. Unless it is exercised, the option will lapse and any premium paid will be lost. Expiry dates may be calculated as follows:

1. For equities. The Wednesday in the last full account period of that calendar month.
2. For the FT-SE 100 Index and gilt options. The last business day of the calendar month.

3. For currency options. The Friday before the third Wednesday in each calendar month.

But *always* check the contract note.

Exercise price

The price at which an option contract gives the holder the right to buy or sell the underlying share is called the 'exercise price'. These exercise prices are fixed by the Stock Exchange which will choose a number of them, some below and some above the market price of the underlying share.

When a new class of traded options is introduced to the market, normally two exercise prices are established for the class: one below and one above the current price of the shares. More than two exercise prices may be introduced where it is felt that there is a possibility of a large price movement in a new stock. For example, GEC call options expiring next January there may be the following exercise prices with GEC share prices at 166p: 140p; 160p; 180p; 200p; 220p; and 240p.

There will always be at least one price above and one price below the current market price of the underlying share. So, in this case we would expect GEC to be trading above 140p but below 240p. If the market price of GEC moves out of this range, then new additional exercise prices will be introduced. This occurs when the share prices close above/below the highest/lowest exercise price for four consecutive days, or if it closes more than half way between the current exercise price and the next to be introduced.

Options on a particular underlying share which have the same expiry date *and* exercise price are known as a 'series'. Puts introduced at the same time would have six similar series.

Introduction of new series

The Council of The Stock Exchange has established a procedure for introducing new series, and, except at an expiry date, new traded stock options series will only be introduced where one of the following criteria is fulfilled:

1. The price of the underlying stock at the close of the traded options market:
   (a) exceeds the highest exercise price in the class on four successive business days; or
   (b) on any business day rises to a level midway between the highest current exercise price in the class, and the exercise price of the next series to be introduced.
2. The price of the underlying stock at the close of the traded options market:
   (a) falls below the lowest exercise price in the class on four successive business days; or

TABLE 1.3 Fixed scale for traded
options on UK equities.

50p	160	390	850
60	180	420	900
70	200	460	950
80	220	500	1,000
90	240	550	1,050
100	260	600	1,100
110	280	650	1,150
120	300	700	1,200 etc.
130	330	750	
140	360	800	

TABLE 1.4 Fixed scale
for traded options on
Vaal Reefs.

US$	
30	90
35	100
40	110
45	120
50	130
60	140
70	150
80	160

(b) on any business day falls to a level midway between the lowest current exercise price in the class and the exercise price of the next series to be introduced.

New exercise prices in series approaching expiry will not normally be introduced within the following timescale:

1. Equity options: During the account in which the expiry of the series concerned takes place.
2. Gilt options: Ten business days prior to expiry.
3. Index options: Ten business days prior to expiry.

Fixed scale for traded options

The fixed scale for traded options on UK equities is as shown in Table 1.3. Traded options on Vaal Reefs have the scale shown in Table 1.4.

Premium

The price of a traded option is known as the 'Premium' and it is quoted in terms of an option on a *single share*. You should remember, however, that the smallest unit traded is one contract (usually 1,000 shares). Thus, if the premium is quoted as 35p, the minimum consideration will be 35p × 1,000, i.e. £350 per contract. Premiums (like share prices) are determined by the forces of supply and demand making themselves felt, in this case, on the trading options exchange.

THE *FINANCIAL TIMES*

In the *Financial Times* details of the traded options market can be found under the section headed 'The London Traded Options'. If you look at the example in Fig. 1.1, you will see that it lists the shares, indexes and gilts (currencies are listed under the section headed 'Currencies, Money and Capital Markets') that may be traded. The title of the underlying security is shown under the heading 'Option', commencing with Allied Lyons through to the FT-SE 100 Index. The shares are grouped together according to the cycle of their expiry dates.

Like shares, traded options have bid and offer prices. All premiums quoted in the *FT* are 'offer' prices, whereas in reality there is usually a substantial 'spread' between the buying and the selling prices. It is important when dealing to know the dealing spread that exists.

In the example, you will see that there are usually three, sometimes four, exercise prices shown. In fact, there are often more options (or series) available than published in the *FT*. The number of different options available in any one class varies widely and will depend on the activity of the underlying security; the more movement in the share price, for example, the more need there will be for a greater number of exercise prices.

In the sample page from the *FT* (Fig. 1.1), you can see the details of options available on Allied Lyons illustrated as follows:

Option	Premium	Calls			Puts		
		Jan	*Apr*	*Jul*	*Jan*	*Apr*	*Jul*
Allied Lyons 345*	330	17	40	47	$1\frac{1}{2}$	17	28
	360	$2\frac{1}{2}$	24	33	18	33	45
	390	3	14	23	48	52	62

*Share price

The first information provided is the underlying share price, in this case 345p. There are two exercise prices above this figure and one below. If the share price was to drop below 330p, an additional series at 300p would be introduced. The other series would still remain in existence until expiry.

LONDON TRADED OPTIONS

Option	CALLS Jan.	CALLS Apr.	CALLS Jul.	PUTS Jan.	PUTS Apr.	PUTS Jul.
Allied Lyons (*345) 330	17	40	47	1½	17	28
360	2½	24	33	18	33	45
390	3	14	23	48	52	62
Brit. Airways (*166) 140	27	33	40	1½	17	28
360	2½	24	33	18	33	45
390	3	14	23	48	52	62
Brit. & Comm. (*334) 330	10	37	50	4	25	35
360	1	23	35	30	50	55
390	1	13	25	60	70	75
B.P. (*252) 220	33	42	50	½	8	14
240	13	26	38	1	16	22
260	2	17	24	11	27	33
Bass (*782) 750	40	80	100	2	27	45
800	5	52	75	23	53	70
850	2	33	55	70	85	100
Cable & Wire (*360) 330	32	52	65	1	17	27
360	6	35	50	6	27	40
390	2	20	37	32	47	55
Cons. Gold (*878) 850	38	110	155	7	70	100
900	8	90	135	35	100	140
950	3	65	110	85	140	175
Courtaulds (*340) 300	43	60	68	½	12	25
330	13	42	53	2	25	38
360	2	27	40	22	40	55
Com. Union (*345) 300	47	58	70	1	16	23
330	17	40	52	2	28	37
360	2	25	40	18	45	52
390	1	14	30	48	65	73
British Gas (*133) 130	5	14	19	1	9	14
135	1	-	-	4	-	-
140	-	10	14	-	16	21
G.E.C. (*157) 140	17	24	32	1	7	9
160	1	12	19	5	15	20
180	½	7	14	25	28	33
G.K.N. (*303) 280	25	45	59	1½	21	28
300	7	34	44	5	31	36
330	1	19	35	30	50	57
Grand Met. (*444) 420	25	45	62	1½	23	33
460	1½	27	43	20	45	53
500	1	13	30	60	73	78
I.C.I. (*1110) 1100	20	83	122	7	80	97
1150	4	60	100	45	110	123
1200	3	43	82	95	142	153
Jaguar (*332) 280	54	65	78	½	12	20
300	34	50	65	½	20	30
330	7	32	47	5	30	40
360	1	20	30	30	52	62
Land Securities (*453) 420	35	62	73	3	12	25
460	3	38	53	11	30	48
500	2	23	35	50	57	75
Marks & Spencer (*178) 160	18	30	34	1½	8	12
180	2	18	22	5	18	24
200	1	10	13	24	30	34
Britoil (*454) 390	67	82	90	1	6	14
420	35	55	67	2	12	23
460	5	30	40	10	30	40
Rolls-Royce (*131) 120	12	21	26	1	11	16
130	4	15	22	3	14	20
140	1	11	18	11	21	27
Sainsbury (*229) 200	30	40	46	1	5	11
220	10	27	33	2	12	18
240	1	16	24	13	23	30
Shell Trans. (*1025) 1000	32	92	120	4	75	92
1050	4	63	97	30	102	118
1100	1	42	77	80	135	147
Storehouse (*254) 240	18	35	48	2	14	23
260	3	24	37	8	23	33
280	2	14	27	27	38	45
Trafalgar House (*329) 300	30	45	53	2	13	23
330	6	28	38	6	25	35
360	3	15	27	35	45	52
T.S.B. (*112) 100	13	18	21	1	4	6
110	4	11	15	2	8	12
120	1	7	10	9	14	17
Woolworth (*252) 240	17	40	50	1	18	23
260	4	25	37	15	27	32
280	2	14	25	35	45	50

Option	CALLS Feb.	CALLS May	CALLS Aug.	PUTS Feb.	PUTS May	PUTS Aug.
LASMO (*313) 280	45	63	75	11	32	42
300	30	50	63	20	42	55
330	20	35	50	37	57	72
P. & O. (*538) 460	87	102	117	4	17	25
500	52	70	85	12	30	43
550	20	45	63	32	58	72
Pilkington (*239) 220	28	43	53	8	18	23
240	18	33	43	18	30	35
260	12	25	33	33	38	45
Plessey (*156) 140	22	30	35	6	10	14
160	10	20	27	14	20	25
180	5½	12	18	29	33	35
Prudential (*844) 800	70	82	107	22	47	58
850	40	60	83	45	68,	85
Racal (*236) 200	40	53	61	3	9	15
220	25	39	49	8	16	22
240	14	29	37	18	24	34
R.T.Z. (*368) 360	30	58	75	20	50	60
380	17	43	-	35	60	-
390	-	-	55	-	-	80
Vaal Reefs (*$103) 90	20	30	37	3	8	13
100	14	23	32	8½	16	19
110	8½	16	25	16	24	30

Option	CALLS Mar.	CALLS Jun.	CALLS Sep.	PUTS Mar.	PUTS Jun.	PUTS Sep.
Amstrad (*137) 120	24	31	37	6	10	14
130	17	25	32	10	14	18
140	12	20	25	14	19	23
Barclays (*490) 420	87	90	102	10	17	27
460	52	67	77	23	35	47
500	27	45	55	45	57	72
Beecham (*459) 420	58	78	87	13	23	35
460	35	55	67	30	42	50
500	19	38	50	55	65	73
Boots (*253) 240	30	37	47	15	22	28
260	18	27	37	23	30	42
280	12	18	-	35	42	-
BTR (*273) 260	29	36	45	12	25	28
280	18	27	35	22	33	38
300	10	19	-	37	45	-
Blue Circle (*419) 390	52	60	72	18	33	43
420	32	47	58	33	48	57
460	15	33	43	58	68	77
Dixons (*185) 180	20	32	40	14	18	25
200	11	23	33	25	30	38
220	6	15	25	42	48	52
Glaxo (*1018) 950	122	160	202	39	64	85
1000	93	130	175	60	87	105
1050	67	110	153	85	112	130
Hawker Sidd. (*473) 460	43	53	70	22	45	55
500	23	37	50	45	72	78
Hansons (*138) 130	15	21	26	4½	8¼	12
140	9½	15	21	9	13	17
Lonrho (*269) 240	36	45	50	10	17	22
260	23	34	39	18	25	30
280	13	22	-	29	35	-
Midland Bk (*388) 360	50	60	72	18	30	37
390	28	45	57	32	42	52
420	15	30	-	55	60	-
Sears (*132) 120	17	23	29	4	8	12
130	11	18	24	8	14	19
140	7	13	19	13	20	24
Tesco (*156) 140	23	30	35	6	10	15
160	14	19	24	13	22	24
180	-	12	17	-	36	36
Trusthouse Forte (*217) 200	23	34	42	10	17	25
220	13	24	33	23	30	35
240	7	16	25	35	42	47
Thorn EMI (*574) 500	93	113	132	10	18	27
550	60	85	98	22	35	45
600	30	57	68	47	62	67
Unilever (*484) 460	52	70	85	23	38	50
500	32	48	70	40	57	70
550	16	33	50	77	90	100
Wellcome (*390) 360	58	70	85	14	30	42
390	38	55	70	30	45	55
420	28	42	58	50	63	73

Option	Feb.	May	Aug.	Feb.	May	Aug.
Conv. 9½% 2005 (*100) 98	-	-	4¼	-	-	2¼
100	-	-	3½	-	-	3¼
102	-	-	2⁹	-	-	4⁹
Tr. 11¼% 1991 (*106) 104	1⅞	-	-	⅛	-	-
106	⁹	-	-	1¼	-	-
108	⁵	-	-	2⅝	-	-
Tr. 12% 1995 (*111) 110	-	2⅛	2½	-	1⅜	2⅛
112	-	1⅛	1½	-	-	3½
Tr. 11¼% 03/07 (*117) 116	1⅞	3¼	-	1½	3⅞	-
118	1	2⅛	-	3	4⅛	-
120	½	1⅝	-	4⅛	5⅛	-

Option		Jan.	Feb.	Mar.	Apr.	Jan.	Feb.	Mar.	Apr.
FT-SE Index (*1760)	1600	165	178	198	220	3	23	40	55
	1650	115	140	165	185	7	35	57	70
	1700	75	105	133	155	18	53	75	92
	1750	40	75	107	130	35	72	100	115
	1800	19	53	85	105	68	100	127	140
	1850	6	37	65	85	110	135	158	170
	1900	3	26	53	70	160	175	195	205

January 19 Total Contracts 24,201 Calls 15,244 Puts 8,957
FT-SE Index Calls 1,460 Puts 961
*Underlying security price.

FIG. 1.1 Example from the *Financial Times*.

These figures show the premiums (offer prices) for each series. Thus, in theory, the price of an option expiring in July to buy one Allied Lyons share (a call option) for 360p would be 33p. In practice, you would need to purchase at least one contract representing 1,000 shares at a cost of £330.

IN-THE-MONEY AND OUT-OF-THE-MONEY

A call option whose exercise price is below the current market price of the underlying security is said to be 'in-the-money'. In the above example with the current share price at 345p, the exercise price of 330p (or any exercise below 345p) is said to be 'in-the-money'. A call option whose exercise price is above the current price of the underlying security is said to be 'out of the money'. In the above example with the current share price at 345p, the exercise prices of 360p and 390p are said to be 'out-of-the-money'. When the share price and the exercise price are the same the option is said to be 'at-the-money'.

Remember the 'exercise price' is the price at which the buyer of a call option may buy the underlying security. In the above example there are three exercise prices quoted at 330p, 360p and 390p.

If you think that the market price of an underlying share in which you are interested is likely to rise over the next few weeks, even months, then you would buy a 'call option'. The extent that you believe the share price will rise and the likely time period involved will, among other factors, govern your choice of options exercise price and series.

SUBMISSION OF ORDERS TO A BROKING FIRM

A client instructing a broking firm to deal on his behalf must give the following information:

1. The number of contracts to be bought or sold.
2. The class of option (i.e. the underlying security and whether it is a call option or a put option).
3. The expiry month and exercise price of the series.
4. Whether the order will open or close a position.
5. Whether, if the order cannot be executed immediately, it is to be entered as a public limit order, and if so, whether it is to be good till cancelled (GTC) or only good for the day (GD).
6. Any other conditions attached to the order (remembering that contingent orders may not be entered as public limit orders).

SUMMARY

We have now looked at the main technical terms and vocabulary used to describe the basic elements of traded options. It is suggested, at this stage, you turn to the 'Glossary' on p. 187 and familiarise yourself with this new 'language'.

TWO

PURCHASING CALL OPTIONS

INTRODUCTION

You will remember that a call option contract confers the right to buy a fixed number of shares at a specific price within a predetermined period of time.

Let us suppose that you have been reading your *FT* carefully and that you are now very optimistic about Commercial Union. You feel, therefore, that it would be a good time a buy a call option in Commercial Union (CU). At the time, the share price of CU is 309p. You must now decide which series is likely to be the most profitable. But before doing that you must ask yourself two important questions: (a) by how *much* will the share price rise? and (b) how *quickly* will the share price rise?

Both the *amount* and the *speed* of any rise in the price of the underlying share will have an effect on the premium prices. Understanding the importance of timing and its effect on option prices is a vital part of success in the traded option market.

Example: Commercial Union

In our example of Commercial Union, let us look at what actually happened during a period of six trading days in July:

Share: Commercial Union
Trading period: 30 June to 7 July
Share price: 309p to 320p

During the trading period above, the share price rose by 11p from 309p to 320p: an increase of 3.5 per cent in six days. On 30 June, the premiums (offer prices) were quoted as follows:

Option	Premium	Calls		
		July	Oct	Jan
CU 309*	280	33	40	—
	300	15	29	35
	330	4	15	24

* share price

By 7 July, the premiums being quoted were as shown below:

Option	Premium	Calls		
		July	Oct	Jan
CU 320*	280	42	49	—
	300	23	35	45
	330	3.5	19	30

*share price

You can now see that, while the CU share price has risen by just over 3.5 per cent, the premiums have moved up by a much larger extent:

280 July series has risen by 27 per cent (33p–42p);
300 July series has risen by 53 per cent (15p–23p);
330 July series has fallen by 12 per cent (4p–3.5p).

The biggest gain available would have been from the 300 July series which has risen by 53 per cent. However, the 330 July series has actually fallen by 12 per cent despite the rise in the underlying share.

Before we look at the factors that affect these option prices, let us look at another example of a purchase of a call option in action.

Example: Courtaulds

At the beginning of September, Courtaulds had attracted a lot of press comment and the reaction was that Courtaulds was currently undervalued, and consequently a cheap stock to purchase. Fund managers had neglected the stock and this gave the traded options investor a good opportunity to purchase some longer-dated call options. Technically, Courtaulds had broken through a critical resistance area of 480p for more than two days and had also penetrated through its recent down trend. So we therefore decided to purchase the Jan 500 calls at 35p (share price 486p). This was therefore a longer-dated 'out of the money' call option.

By 1 October the premium had reached 60p (bid) to give the investor a profit of 25p, or 71 per cent in two weeks!

So we must now look at the factors that affect these option prices and why the 300 July series and others have risen, whereas the 330 July series has fallen.

CALL OPTION PREMIUMS

The relationship between the exercise price and the share price is one of the main factors that will influence the movement of option premiums. In the above example for CU, there were three exercise prices available: 280p, 300p and 330p. This meant that on 30 June, when CU stood at 309p, the purchaser of a call option could have the option to buy CU at either 280p, 300p or 330p (in return for paying a premium). If the investor opts for the 280 series, then clearly the right to buy CU at 280p when the share price already stands at 309p must be worth at least 29p (309p – 280p = 29p).

This part of the premium is known as the 'intrinsic value'.

You will see that when CU was standing at 309p, premiums for both the 280 series and the 300 series had intrinsic values, whereas the 330 series had no intrinsic value. Although the premiums for the 330 series had no intrinsic value they still carried a price or justified a value: this part of the premium is known as a 'time value'.

The more time there is left before expiry of an option, the higher will be the premium. Thus in June, for example, the July 330 series will be cheaper than the following January 330 series.

We have seen, therefore, that each premium may be made up of two elements: 'intrinsic value' and 'time value'.

Some premiums will contain a measure of both elements; some may have no intrinsic value, as we have seen, while all premiums immediately prior to expiry will have little or no time value.

In-the-money and out-of-the-money calls

In the CU example, certain options had intrinsic values while others only had time values. This characteristic will determine how the options (more accurately – the series) are categorised. As in Chapter One, all options are defined as either (a) 'in-the-money'; (b) 'out-of-the-money'; or (c) 'at-the-money'.

To refresh your memory, 'in-the-money' call options are where the exercise price of the option is *below* the share price, e.g. CU's existing share price of 309p has 'in-the-money options' in the 280 and 300 series. 'Out-of-the-money' call options are where the exercise price of the option is *above* the share price – in the CU example, the 330 series. 'At-the-money' call options are where the exercise price of the option is the *same* as the share price. In the CU example, an 'at-the-money' option does not exist.

As the underlying share price is seldom static for very long, changes in the share price can mean changes to the category of an option. In our example, if the share price instead of rising to 320p had fallen to 295p, what was an in-the-money option (300 series) would have become an out-of-the-money option. This change that occurs when options either gain or lose intrinsic value had a marked effect on the pricing of premiums.

Time value

As options have a finite life, the period left before expiry will have an impact on

TABLE 2.1 Intrinsic and time values of
Commerical Union.

Commercial Union at 309p	Intrinsic	Time	Total
280 July	29	4	33
280 Oct	29	11	40
300 July	9	6	15
300 Oct	9	20	29
300 Jan	9	26	35
330 July	0	4	4
330 Oct	0	15	15
330 Jan	0	24	24

the premium. As the expiry date approaches, so the time value of the option becomes progressively less, until at expiry the time value is nil. Time value is that part of the premium which is over and above the intrinsic value (if any). In our example of CU, the intrinsic and time values were made up as shown in Table 2.1.

Purchasers of the call options in Table 2.1 are therefore buying time: as time progresses, so the time value of the premium is gradually eroded, until at expiry the time value is nil.

So time works *against the buyer* of call options.

As can be seen, time values for the Jan series are worth more than those for the preceding Oct series. Obviously, the longer the option, the greater chance there is of the underlying share price rising. Consequently, the investor has to pay a higher premium for this advantage of extra time. The longer the expiry date selected, the less dramatically will the premium react to share price moves: the nearer the expiry, the more dramatic the premium moves. The most conservative position would be in-the-money longest expiry; the most aggressive, out-of-the-money nearest expiry.

Volatility

One factor, which is fundamental to the pricing of an option, is the 'volatility' of the share price. This is the market's expectation of how volatile share movements in the particular company will be during the life of the option. Volatility is one factor which is not readily available to the investor, although it can be determined in one of two ways:

1. By analysing the past movements of the share price to determine the historic volatility over any chosen time period.
2. By calculating back from the option premium the implied volatility of the option. That is the volatility figure which is built into the pricing of an option premium.

Theoretically, options maturing at a specific date should have an identical implied volatility for each of the different strike prices. In practice, this is rarely the case. The option trader can use this fact to his advantage by choosing the option strike price which shows the lowest implied volatility, if he believes that the other factors and his outlook for the movements in the underlying share price would allow him to make a profit.

Summary

In our CU example, we saw that the premiums of some options had gained in value while others had actually declined. The first observation we can now make is that the premiums of the in-the-money options increased, while the out-of-the-money options decreased in value. The reasons for this are now also obvious. When the share price rises slowly over a period of time, any time value will be gradually eroded away. This in turn will reduce the value of out-of-the money options, since in these options the investor has only paid a premium for time-value. When the share price rises slowly over a period of time, it will favour those options that have intrinsic value, i.e. in-the-money options.

Example: Commercial Union

Using Commercial Union again as an example, let us this time see what happened to the option premiums when CU's share price moved up from 267p on 2 October to 286p on 22 October:

Option	Premium	Calls			Option	Premium	Calls		
		Oct	Jan	Apr			Oct	Jan	Apr
CU 267*	260	17	28	38	CU 286*	260	28	38	48
2 October	280	7	18	28	22 October	280	8	27	37
	300	2	11	18		300	1	17	24
	330	1	6	13		330	1	8	15

*Share price

You will see that CU's share price has risen by nearly 7 per cent (267p to 286p) during the period. During the same period, the option premiums have changed significantly. A glance at those series expiring in October will illustrate some of the points made earlier:

   260 Oct has increased by 64 per cent (17p–28p);
   280 Oct has increased by 14 per cent (7p–8p);
   300 Oct has fallen by 50 per cent (2p–1p);
   330 Oct has remained the same.

So while the share price has risen by 7 per cent, the 260 Oct series (in-the-money option) has shown a dramatic increase. The 280 Oct series, originally an out-of-the-money option, attracted some intrinsic value as the share price moved up and the option increased in value. The remaining options were out-of-the-money and showed either a fall or remained static.

This example serves to demonstrate that if an investor believes that the price of the underlying share will increase, but only gradually during the period the option has to run, then he should purchase in-the-money options. Out-of-the-money options need a more dramatic movement in the share price in order to realise a profit on the premiums paid.

Using Consolidated Goldfields to illustrate out-of-the-money options

Again let us look at the period from 2 October to 22 October:

Option	Premium	Calls			Option	Premium	Calls		
		Oct	Jan	Apr			Oct	Jan	Apr
ConsGold 579 *	500	82	97	110	ConsGold 672 *	500	173	187	198
2 October	550	37	73	77	22 October	550	125	144	162
	600	16	37	50		600	75	115	130
	650	—	—	—		650	28	87	100

* Share price

The share price has increased from 579p to 672p, an increase of 16 per cent. The option premiums have risen as follows:

   500 Oct series has risen by 110 per cent (82p–173p);
   550 Oct series has risen by 237% (37p–125p);
   600 Oct series has risen by 368% (16p–75p).

In this example the out-of-the-money options have shown the largest percentage increases, i.e. 600 series showing a 368 per cent increase.

So, if the investor feels that the share price is going to increase dramatically over a short period, e.g. due to a takeover bid speculation, then he should opt for out-of-the-money options. By achieving the greatest percentage gain, he will also be operating with the maximum gearing.

Using Consolidated Goldfields to illustrate in-the-money and out-of-the-money premiums

Let us use the ConsGold example again to see how the in-the-money and out-of-the-money premiums are made up.

The share price of ConsGold on 2 October was 579p and the 500 Oct series had a premium of 82p. So, the right to buy ConsGold at 500p (remember that call options give the investor the right to buy shares in the underlying security) when the share price is already standing at 579p *must* be worth at least 79p (579p–500p). This 79p is, we know, the 'intrinsic value' of the premium.

The remaining 3p is, of course, the 'time value'. This represents the amount that buyers are prepared to pay in the hope that the share price will rise before expiry date – in this case, less than a month away.

To summarise, on 2 October:

ConsGold share price   = 579p
500 Oct series premium = 82p
Intrinsic value 79p + time value 3p = 82p

You should now look at the ConsGold 600 Oct series which on 2 October was an out-of-the-money option. You will see that the premium is made up entirely of time value.

Clearly, the longer the option has to run, the greater will be the time value attached to the premium. You should now compare the 500 Oct and the 500 Jan series. Although the exercise price is the same, there is a difference in the premiums.

Option	Calls	
	Oct	Jan
500	82	97

Why the difference?

As the exercise price (500p) and the share price (579p) are the same in both cases, the intrinsic value (79p) is also the same. The time values are, however, different and the investor is paying an extra 15p for the Jan expiry date:

500 Oct 82p (79p + 3p);
500 Jan 97p (79p + 18p).

Because the 500 Jan series has a further three months to run, the share price has a greater opportunity to rise. For this benefit the investor has to pay an extra premium, or increased time value.

The nearer an option is to expiry, the less time value will be attached to the premium until, at expiry, time value will be nil. Hence, out-of-the-money options at expiry are worth nothing and in-the-money options at expiry have only intrinsic value attached to their premiums.

You should now be able to see at a glance whether any option is in- or out-of-the-money and be able to calculate the various components, intrinsic values and time values. Select a number of examples from the list of traded options in the *FT* to make sure you understand the make up of any call option premium. In the next chapter we will move on to 'put options'.

CRITERIA SUMMARY FOR BUYING CALL OPTIONS

Anticipate rapid move upwards = Near dated out-of-money options
Gradual move upwards = Near/medium-term in-the-money options

Let's take another example of a 'call' option in practice.

At the beginning of September 1987, Consolidated Goldfields had been highlighted in the press with much speculation on the possibility of a bid from Ivanhoe, a ConsGold bid for Newmont or a Newmont bid for ConsGold. Whatever the outcome, there was considerable interest in the ConsGold share price and in the options market. This, together with the possibility of a further increase in the price of gold, led us to believe that we could see further upwards movement on the ConsGold share price.

Technically, (on the charts) ConsGold had broken through its down trend and the share price had also moved up through its 20-day moving average which itself had started to move up, confirming a 'buy' indicator.

So, we decided to be fairly aggressive and go for the Jan 1,450 calls at 125p (offered). This is an out-of-the-money option with the ConsGold share price standing at 1,395p. Again, the idea here is to provide us with high gearing and good potential profits. Within a week the ConsGold share price stood at nearly 1,500p and the 1,450 Jan calls could then be sold for 175p (bid) to give you a profit of 40 per cent!

TIME CHARTS AND CALL OPTIONS

Now we have examined in some detail the make up of premiums relating to call options, let's look briefly at some time charts that illustrate the behaviour of call option premiums.

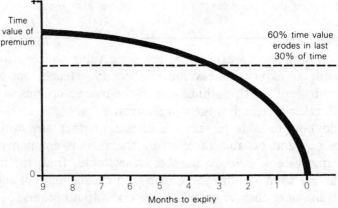

FIG. 2.1 Decay of time value over a nine-month period.

We have already seen that time value is eroded as an option moves towards its expiry date. The important point to remember, <u>however, is that time value does</u> <u>not</u> decay at any even rate. Figure 2.1 illustrates the <u>typical pattern over nine</u> <u>months and you can see how, initially, time value declines very slowly until after</u> <u>five months when the decrease is far more rapid.</u>

<u>This important principle will apply over shorter time scales: e.g. over one</u> <u>month the decline will be much more rapid in the last two weeks.</u> Let us see now how this principle works in practice by using two further examples of Commercial Union.

Commercial Union: July 280

Figure 2.2 illustrates how the Commercial Union July 280 calls costing 33p premium are made up of 4p 'time value' and 29p 'intrinsic value'. The time value erodes to zero as the expiry date approaches.

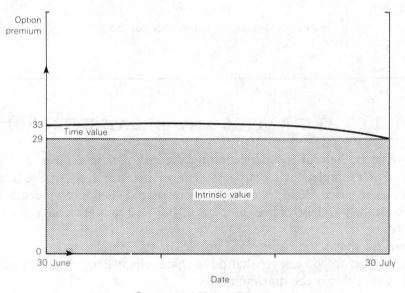

FIG. 2.2 Commercial Union: July 280 calls.

Commercial Union: October 280

Let's now look at a longer-dated option in an October cycle. 'Time value' now has a *greater* value, since the October options have more time to run than the July options.

Time value:	11p
Intrinsic value:	29p
Total cost:	40p

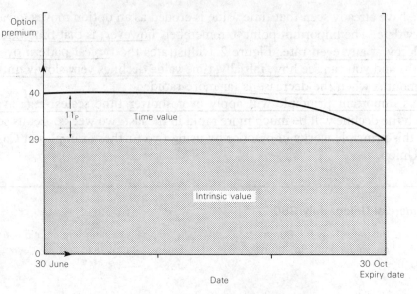

FIG. 2.3 Commercial Union: October 280 calls.

RISK/REWARD RATIOS AND BREAK-EVEN POINTS

Graphs can be helpful in understanding the risk/reward ratio of any specific option. For example, let us suppose that an investor feels that Commercial Union's share price (309p) is going to increase and therefore he decides to go ahead with the purchase of five contracts of July 280 calls at an offer price of 33p on 30 June.

Figure 2.4 shows the risk/reward profile for this purchase.

From the graph you can see that if the share falls to 280p the entire premium of 33p is lost: this is the maximum loss.

Maximum loss = Premium paid

At a share price of 313p, where the intrinsic value equals the cost of the premium paid, the investor reaches a break-even situation.

Break-even = Exercise price + Premium (280p + 33p = 313p)

A profit occurs when the share price increases to a figure above 313p.

On 25 July the shares have risen to 325p. So our investor made the correct decision and the calls now have an intrinsic value of 45p (325p – 280p). Since there is a little time value left as well, say 2p, the call option is worth 47p. So the

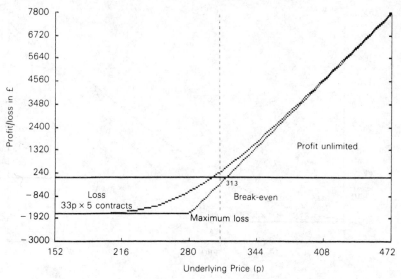

FIG. 2.4 Commercial Union security strategy: July 280 calls.

investor sells his calls on 25 July for 47p, making him a profit of 14p per contract (47p – 33p).

The results of the transactions are as follows:

Purchase of five contracts at 33p each = 1,650p
Sale of five contracts at 47p each = 2,350p
Net profit before expenses = £700 (14p per contract × 1,000)

The investor has realised a 43 per cent return on his investment on a 5 per cent move in the underlying security.

If our investor decided to wait until expiry and the share price remained unchanged, as it did in this case, then his profit would be 12p per contract (325p – 280p = 45p – original premium paid (33p) = 12p).

At expiry there is no time value attached to the premium, but the investor *must* always close (in this case sell) the options he has purchased, otherwise he will not receive the premiums due to him.

Let's now look at a graph showing the risk/reward profile for buying a longer-dated call: the October 280 calls at 40p (Fig. 2.5) – date, 30 June; share price, 309p.

Again, the investor feels that the Commercial Union share price is going to increase but thinks that it will have a slower growth. He therefore decides on the October expiry cycle, allowing extra time for an increase in the share price.

The cost of buying extra time is reflected in the option premium. In this example the 280 October series cost 40p. (The July 280 series cost 33p.) The investor is paying an extra seven pence for this extra time value. The investor

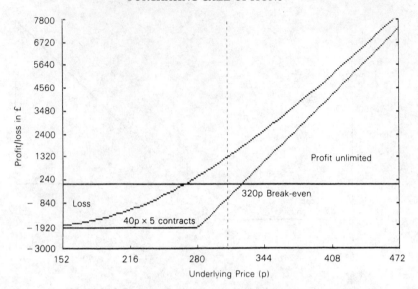

FIG. 2.5 Commercial Union security strategy: October 280 calls.

goes ahead with the purchase of five contracts of the October 280 calls at a price of 40p. Let us look at the risk/reward profile and the break-even point for this transaction by studying Fig. 2.5.

From the graph you can see that at a share price of 280p the entire premium of 40p is lost: this is the maximum loss.

Maximum loss = premium paid (40p)

When the share price reaches a value equal to the exercise price of 280p plus the cost of the premium 40p, the investor achieves a break-even situation. At expiry, the intrinsic value of the option must equal the exercise price plus the premium.

Break-even = Exercise price + Premium paid (280p + 40p = 320p)

A profit occurs on the option when the share price increases to a figure in excess of 320p (280p + 40p). On 25 July the share price has risen to 315p and, because our investor was still losing money until he reached his break-even point at 320p, the investor decided not to sell at that point. In October, just prior to expiry, the shares had risen to 350p. The calls now have an intrinsic value of 70p (350p – 280p) but no time value. The call option is now worth 70p.

The investor sells his calls for 70p, making a profit of 30p per contract (70p – original premium paid (40p) = 30p).

The results of the transaction are as follows:

Purchase of five contracts at 40p each = 2,000p
Sale of five contracts at 70p each = 3,500p
Net profit before expenses = £1,500 (30p per contact × 1,000)

The investor has realised a 75 per cent return on his investment on a 13 per cent move in the underlying security.

These examples show how you can quickly assess first the break-even point for any contract premium and then the share price needed for a particular return on your investment. This sort of calculation will help you decide on which series to choose and also when to sell your call option.

FT-SE 100 INDEX

The FT-SE 100 Index (known as 'Footsie' in the market) was introduced in January 1984 in order to provide investors with an indicator of equity price movements during trading hours.

An index is a measure of the value of a group of stocks. The base may be adjusted occasionally to reflect changes in the capitalisation of the group, in order to maintain continuity when some stocks are added to or dropped from the index group. Consequently, the index level will only change as a result of price changes during trading.

The purpose of the index options is to enable the investor to profit, or protect himself against price movements in the stock market, rather than individual securities. So by the use of the FT-SE Traded Options Index, the investor can now take a course of action to protect his portfolio or to express a view of the overall market, without the necessity of dealing in individual stocks.

Selection

The Council of The Stock Exchange consulted with traders involved with traded options and agreed that options should be traded on the FT-SE 100 Share Index. The choice of securities underlying this index and its subsequent monitoring are the responsibility of the Steering Committee, comprising major financial associations as well as The Stock Exchange and the *Financial Times*. Characteristics of the index are as follows:

1. Its base value was established on 3 January 1984 at, 1,000.0, and is calculated to one decimal place and updated at one minute intervals during business hours.
2. It is based on 100 of the largest companies and covers a wide range of securities. It is thus capable of tracking the market as a whole.
3. It is based on a weighted arithmetic formula, so that changes in the value of the index correlate with changes in the values of portfolios.

Expiry date

At any time index option contracts are available with one, two, three and four months to expiry. Unlike traded options on stocks, traded options on the FT-SE Index expire on the last business day of these months.

Exercise prices

These are of intervals of 25 index points up to a level of 1,700 points. New series introduced above 1,700 are at intervals of 50 index points.

New series are only introduced in the following circumstances:

1. Where the index closes on two consecutive days above or below the highest or lowest exercise price currently available.
2. Where on any day the index closes either (a) at or above a level midway between the highest currently available exercise price and the next one due to be introduced, or (b) at or below a level midway between the lowest currently available exercise price and the next one due to be introduced.

Underlying value of the index option contract

Each contract comprises 1,000 units of 1p each, therefore each contract represents a value of £10 multiplied by the index exercise price. This means that the 1,100 series has an underlying value of £11,000.

Quotation

The premium for each series is quoted in pence per unit of the contract and thus a premium of 30p per unit represents a cost of £300 per contract. The smallest permitted price fraction in index operation bargains is $\frac{1}{2}$p.

Exercise

This takes place on a cash basis, unlike the account basis used for stock options. It does not involve settlement of an underlying stock through TALISMAN (see Glossary). Automatic exercise occurs on expiry day for in-the-money expiring FT-SE 100 option contracts for market-makers only. For non-market-makers, settlement takes place two business days after the submission of exercise notices. The settlement consideration is the 'in-the-money' element and is calculated by reference to the difference to the index value on the day of exercise and the striking price of the series being exercised, multiplied by £10.

Exercise is available on each day of an account, up to and including the day of expiry.

Calculation of the value of the index upon expiry

Except on expiry days the index value is calculated at 3.40 p.m. on each day. Where exercise takes place on expiry day the index value is determined by taking the average of each of the index values between 11.10 a.m. and 11.20 a.m., after ignoring the highest and lowest values between these times.

The distinction between an exercise at expiry and an exercise at any other time is made to accommodate dealers and clients with open positions in both the options and futures markets.

Dealings on the day of expiry cease at 11.20 a.m.

If normal price collection is impossible on an expiry day then the expiry value will be calculated from the latest 11 index values available before price collection ceased.

Submission of exercise notices to LOCH

Exercise notices have to be physically submitted to the London Options Clearing House (LOCH) by 4.00 p.m. No telephone calls will be accepted as valid exercise instructions. On the last business day of each month, exercise notices relating to these index options series expiring at 11.20 a.m. will be accepted by LOCH until 6.00 p.m.

Position limits

The maximum number of index option contracts permitted to be held or written by a single party, or several parties acting in concert is 20,000 per class.

Margin

1. Public order members: The margin required is 12.5 per cent of the underlying value (i.e. index value × £10) plus or minus the in- or out-of-the-money element, with a minimum margin of two per cent of the underlying value.
2. Market-makers: Calculated on the same basis as applies to 'Traded Options on Stocks', Stock Exchange rules, Section XI.

At the base date, the index comprised 69 industrial stocks, five oils, 21 financial companies, two investment trusts, two mining finance companies and one overseas trader accounting for nearly 70 per cent of the total market value of all UK equities.

Portfolio managers constantly make use of the FT-SE 100 Index to protect their portfolios. For instance, in a falling market they will be writing (selling) call options. In this way any loss suffered from a fall in the value of shares in a portfolio will be covered by the premium received from the written calls.

Alternatively the fund manager can buy 'puts' instead of selling calls to protect his portfolio. (Buying puts and writing options will be covered in more detail in Chapters Three and Five.)

Operation of the Footsie

We will now look at how the Footsie contract works.

Towards the end of October the Footsie index stood at 1,610. An investor who anticipated a rise in the market might have bought a January 1,625 call at 40p.

Each contract of the FT-SE represents a notational value of £10 multiplied by the index value. So, each premium is quoted in pence per unit of 1p × index. In this case, the total premium payable would be £400 (1,000 × premium (40p)) plus expenses.

If at expiry the index stood at 1,700 the investor could exercise his option and would receive the difference between £17,000 and £16,250, i.e. £750, or a net gain of £350 after the deduction of £400 premium paid.

The principal difference between index and stock options is the feature of cash settlement. Whilst dealing in the index, only *money* changes hands, whereas, if a stock option is exercised, it requires delivery of the underlying security.

Intrinsic/time values of index options

Intrinsic and time values operate in the same way with index options as with share options.

For example, let us assume that on 1 July our investor purchased one September 1,100 call option contract at 33p. (The total cost was therefore £330, plus expenses.) On 15 August the index stood at 1,180 and the premium at 85p. The intrinsic value was therefore 80, and the time value 5p. If the investor should now exercise his option he would lose his time value of 5p.

By 25 September the index had increased to 1,220 and the premium was quoted at 118p–123p (bid/offer). At this point, time value was nil and the investor could, at expiry, exercise his option. Unlike stock options, the investor is then entitled to cash as follows:

Holder exercises option and is entitled to:

	£12,200	(1,220 × £10)
less	£11,000	(1,100 × £10)
	£1,200	

You will see that this amount is almost equivalent to the bid premium quotation. So, if 120p was the premium and the investor had sold just prior to expiry, he would have received 120p × 1,000 = £1,200, the same as his entitlement had he exercised his option.

Use of the Footsie

For the investor, a significant movement in share prices can be seen as an opportunity or as an additional risk. As share markets have become more volatile, so investors will look for ways to take advantage of these swings or to protect their investments. The Footsie option provides such opportunities. It enables investors to do the following:

1. Hedge against the risk to their investments.
2. Take a speculative position on the market as a whole.

The various techniques applied to the Footsie to accomplish these two main functions are dealt with later in the book (see pp.42, 52, 74–5 and 91–4).

Before leaving the FT-SE, let's take another example of using the FT-SE in the traded options market.

On 17 September, the FT-SE stood at 2,264 and at this time the market was becoming resilient to the knock-on effects from Wall Street. Also, the recent retail figures published, close to economic forecasts, helped boost confidence in the City. Technically, the market needed to penetrate the 2,298 resistance level, and, if it could manage this, we would step in there and buy some calls. The chart for FT-SE 100 demonstrated that again the recent downtrend had been broken. So we decided to purchase the out-of-the-money 2,400 Oct calls at 17p. Again, within a week, the market had moved up to 2,336 and the October 2,400 calls could now be sold for 117 per cent profit (37p bid).

GILT OPTIONS

A traded option on an equity gives a right to buy (or sell) a specific number of shares (normally 1,000). A traded option on a gilt-edged stock gives the right to buy (or sell) a fixed quantity (£50,000) of a specific gilt-edged stock. The use of traded options in gilts is particularly useful for hedging against sudden movements in interest rates.

If the investor feels that interest rates are going to fall, he can buy call options in gilts and benefit from the increased price of gilt-edged stocks. Similarly, if the investor feels that interest rates are going to rise, he can purchase put options in gilts to protect his portfolio.

So, the investor can see that there is a direct relationship between interest rates and gilt-edged prices. Naturally, supply and demand also has an effect on gilt-edged prices. The following is a list of features of gilt options:

1. Contract size: £50,000 nominal of exchequer 10 per cent 1989.
2. Exercise prices: Two-point intervals (e.g. 98, 100, 102).
3. Option series: Three-, six- and nine-month cycles.
4. Expiry: On the last business day of the month.
5. Premiums: Quoted in terms of points and 32nds of a point. The minimum fluctuation is $\frac{1}{32}$ of a point.

Example 1: Purchasing call options

Options		Calls		
	Nov	Feb	May	
Treasury 11$\frac{3}{4}$ 1991 Gilt price £102	2.$\frac{1}{4}$	2.$\frac{13}{16}$	3.$\frac{1}{4}$	100

The figures above illustrate the 100 and 102 Nov, Feb and May series for the Treasury 11$\frac{3}{4}$ 1991.

So, the investor could purchase an 'in-the-money' call option November 100 series for 2.$\frac{1}{4}$1991. Since the minimum price movement for the premium is $\frac{1}{342}$ (0.03125) per £100, (£15.625 per contract), the buyer of a gilt option which was quoted as 2.25 would have to pay a premium of £1,125 per contract.

Figure 2.6 illustrates the purchase of a Treasury 11$\frac{3}{4}$ call for 2.$\frac{1}{4}$ points.

$$\text{Maximum loss} = 2.\tfrac{1}{4} \text{ points}$$
$$\text{Breakeven} = 100 + 2.\tfrac{1}{4} = 102.\tfrac{1}{4}$$

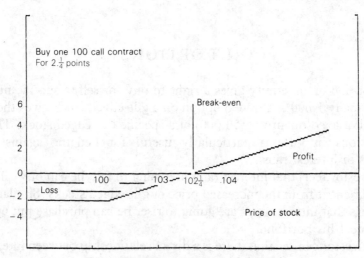

FIG. 2.6 Purchase of a Treasury 11$\frac{3}{4}$ call.

Example 2: Purchasing gilt options

One option price fluctuation represents one per cent of contract size, i.e. one per cent of 50,000 = £500. Thus, each minimum move of $\frac{1}{32}$ or (0.03125) in the option price is worth £15,625.

TABLE 2.2 Treasury 11.$\frac{3}{4}$ 1991: purchase of gilt options.

	Bid	Ask
104	0.06	0.11
106	0.02	0.07
108	0.02	0.03
Nov 110	0.01	0.02
Calls 112	—	0.01

To buy one contract of the Nov 108 calls, offer price 0.03, would cost the investor 0.03 × £500 = £150. See Table 2.2.

Short gilt option contract specification

The following is a list of features of short gilt options:

1. Contract size: £50,000 nominal.
2. Delivery stock: treasury 11$\frac{3}{4}$ per cent 1991.
3. Exercise price: Plus or minus accrued, as for all short gilt stocks.
4. Range of exercise prices: Two point intervals.
5. Exercise timing: Continuous.
6. Option series: Three-, six- and nine-month calls and puts.
7. Expiry: Last business day in February or May or August or November.
8. Minimum premium movement: $\frac{1}{32}$ (value £15.625).
9. Margin: Writer to provide 5 per cent of nominal value plus or minus the in- or out-of-the-money element.
10. Trading hours: 9.05 a.m. to 3.40 p.m.

CURRENCY OPTIONS

The nature of the contract

Underlying security
Traded options are listed by The Stock Exchange on the following currencies:

£ sterling (quoted in US Dollars)

£ sterling (quoted in Deutschmarks)
£ sterling (quoted in French Francs)
Deutschmarks (quoted in US Dollars)

Expiry date

Currency options expire at 6.00 p.m. on the Friday before the third Wednesday of March, June, September and December plus the remaining two of the nearest three months. There are, therefore, six dates trading simultaneously.

Settlement upon expiry takes place on the Wednesday following the third Friday in the month.

Exercise

Currency options are continuously exercisable. Settlement upon exercise takes place 72 hours after the submission of exercise notices. Exercise is available until 6.00 p.m. on expiry days, while on normal trading days exercise is allowable only until 5.00 p.m.

Exercise fee

£20 per exercise transaction in each series plus 30p per contract up to a maximum of £240 per day.

Commission

Commission on currency options is chargeable at the broker's discretion.

Position limits

The maximum number of contracts that may be held or written by a single party or parties acting in concert is 10,000 in any one class.

Margin

For client and public order members the minimum margin required is 8 per cent of the currency value of the underlying contract, plus or minus the amount by which the option is in- or out-of-the-money.

For market-makers the margin is 130 per cent of the daily closing premium value on all *net* positions.

Trading hours

Trading in currency options takes place between the hours of 9.00 a.m. and 3.40 p.m.

Introduction of new series

New series in currency options will be introduced where the underlying currency either exceeds the second highest exercise price currently available or falls below the second lowest currently available.

Sterling contracts

Underlying value
This is £12,500.

Quotation
The premium of each series is quoted in cents, DM or francs per unit of the contract.
   The smallest permitted fractions are as follows:

1. In the case of the $/£ contract, five hundredths of a US cent (i.e. US $0.0005 × 12,500 = $6.25).
2. In the case of the DM/£ contract, one hundredth of a Deutschmark (e.g. DM0.001 × 12,500 = DM12.50).
3. In the case of the French franc/£ contract, five hundredths of a franc (i.e. Fr0.005 × 12,500 = Fr6.25).

Delivery timing
Delivery occurs on the third business day following the submission of the exercise notice.

Delivery
A purchaser of sterling delivers dollars, French francs or Deutschmarks to a bank nominated by ICCH via his clearing member. A seller of sterling delivers the sterling to a bank nominated by ICCH.

Deutschmark contracts

Underlying value
This is DM62,500.

Exercise prices
These are quoted in US cents and are introduced at intervals of one cent.

Quotation
The premium of each series is quoted in cents per unit of the contract. The smallest permitted price fraction is one hundredth of a US cent (i.e. US$0.0001 × 62,500 = $6.25).

Delivery
A purchaser of a Deutschmark option delivers dollars to a bank nominated by ICCH via his clearing member. A seller of the currency delivers the specified amount of that currency to a bank nominated by ICCH.

Currencies used for protecting a portfolio

If an investor wished to protect his portfolio, say US$ cash deposits, against a rise in sterling, he would buy sterling calls.

Example

Exchange rate at purchase: $1.40
Premium cost: $0.079 (7.9 cents)
Expiry: Nine months
Contract: Ten contracts
Contract cost: 10 × 12,500 × 0.079 = £9,875

Let's now look at the position two months later:

Exchange rate at sale of calls: $1.45
Option premium: 11.20 cents (intrinsic value 5 cents, time value 6.2 cents)
Contract size: 10 × 12,500 × 0.112 = $14,000

TABLE 2.3 Example of option premiums (spot rate of sterling stands at $1.2550).

Calls	Premiums	Intrinsic value	Time value
Sept 120	7.60	5.50	2.10
Sept 125	5.00	0.50	4.50
Sept 130	3.05	—	3.05
Dec 120	8.90	5.50	3.40
Dec 125	6.45	0.50	5.95
Dec 130	4.55	—	4.55

See Table 2.3 for an example of option premium.

The higher the spot price in relation to the exercise price of the option, the greater the intrinsic value of a call option and the larger the premium payable for it.

THREE

PURCHASING PUT OPTIONS

INTRODUCTION

Purchasing 'put' options is, of course, the *opposite* to purchasing call options. 'Put' options allow the investor to 'sell' shares at an agreed price (i.e. to *put* them on to a new owner).

The purchase of put options is used to take advantage of a *downward* market or share movement. In general, a *decrease* in the price of a stock results in an *increase* in the price of a put option premium. A *call option* is purchased when one is *optimistic* about the future price rise on a stock, whereas a *put option* is purchased when one is *pessimistic* about the stock price and believes that it is going to fall.

For the serious investor, the skilful use of put options clearly increases the number of strategies open to him. As a *decrease* in the market price of the stock can subsequently result in an *increase* in the premium of a put option, it can be sold or exercised at a profit. A clear understanding of this reverse arithmetic is absolutely essential to an understanding of put options and their uses.

Let us assume that you have been reading your *FT* and that you are now pessimistic about Allied Lyons. You feel, therefore, it would be a good time to buy a put option in Allied Lyons, whose share price is 341p. You must now decide which series is likely to be the most profitable. But before doing this, remember to ask yourself those two important questions: a) by how *MUCH* will the share price fall? and b) how *QUICKLY* will the share price fall?

Both the *amount* and *speed* of any fall in the price of the underlying share will have an effect on premium prices. Understanding the importance of timing and its effect on option prices will prove a vital part of your success in the traded options market.

Using Allied Lyons as an example

The following example of Allied Lyons illustrates what actually happened from 2 July to

4 July. During this two-day trading period the share price fell by 5p from 341p to 336p: a fall of 1.5 per cent. On 2 July the premiums (offer prices) were quoted as follows:

Option	Premium		Puts		Option	Premium		Puts	
		July	Oct	Jan			July	Oct	Jan
Allied Lyons 341 *					Allied Lyons 336 *				
2 July	300	1	5	10	4 July	300	1	6	10
	330	4	17	20		330	8	20	23
	360	23	27	32		360	30	35	40

*Share price

You can now see that while the Allied Lyons share price has *fallen* by approximately 1.5 per cent the premiums have *risen* by a much larger extent:

300 July series has remained the same (1p–1p);
330 July series has risen by 100 per cent (4p–8p);
360 July series has risen by 30 per cent (23p–30p).

So, whilst the stock has fallen by 1.5 per cent, the 330 July series has increased by 100 per cent! The 300 July series has remained the same.

PUT OPTION PREMIUMS

As in Chapter Two, when we looked at the factors that affected call option premiums, we can now look at those same factors affecting the put option premiums.

Again, the relationship between the exercise price and the share price is one of the main factors that influence the movement of option premiums. In our example of Allied Lyons, there were three exercise prices available: 300p, 330p and 360p. This meant that on 2 July when Allied Lyons stood at 341p, the purchaser of a put option could have the option to *sell* Allied Lyons at either 300p, 330p or 360p (in return for paying a premium).

If investors opt for the 360 series, then clearly the right to sell Allied Lyons at 360p when the share price stands at 341p must be worth at least 19p (360p – 341p = 19p). We know that this part of the premium is the intrinsic value, as this is an in-the-money option. So you can now begin to understand how put options work. They are the reverse of call options:

Call option purchases: share price rises: premium rises.
Put option purchases: share price falls: premium rises.

When Allied Lyons was standing at 341p, premiums for the 360 July series had intrinsic value, whereas the 300 and 330 series had no intrinsic value – since the right to sell Allied Lyons at 300 or 330, when it was already above these prices, i.e. 341p, cannot have any intrinsic value attached to the premium.

Although the premiums for the 300 and 330 series had no intrinsic value, they still carried a price or justified a value; this part of the premium we already know is the time value. The more time there is left before expiry of an option, the higher will be the premium. Thus in June, for example, the July 300 series will be cheaper than the October 300 series. We have therefore seen (as in Chapter Two with call options) that each premium may be made up of two elements: '*intrinsic value*' and '*time value*'.

In-the-money and out-of-the-money puts

With the Allied Lyons share at 336p, a put option with an exercise price of 360 is 'in-the-money', since the right to sell these shares at 360p when the share price currently stands at 336p, has an intrinsic value of 24p (360p – 336p) and time value of 6p, making the total premium 30p (24p + 6p).

In contrast, the 330 July series is 'out-of-the-money', since there is no intrinsic value attached to the premium of 8p at an exercise price of 330p, when the share price is already at 336p. Remember the 'put option' confers the right to *sell*, so a 'put' is *in-the-money* when the share price is *below* the exercise price, and '*out-of-the-money*' when the share price is *above* the exercise price.

Worked examples: in-the-money put option

Example 1

Share: Allied Lyons (see Fig. 3.1)
Date: 4 July
Share price: 336p.

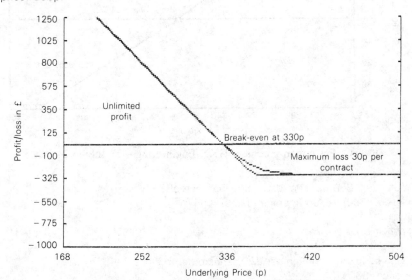

FIG. 3.1 Put option purchase: Allied Lyons – July 360 at 30p.

Maximum loss: 30p per contract at striking (exercise) price of 360p, at expiry
Break-even: 360 − 30p = 330p

Example 2

Share: GKN Engineering (see Fig. 3.2)
Trading period: 17 July to 24 July
Share price: 353p to 330p

During this seven-day trading period the share price fell by 23p from 353p to 330p; a fall of 6.5 per cent.

Break-even risk reward graphs for in-the-money puts

GKN September 390 series puts
See Fig. 3.2.

OPENING CONTRACT
    Date: 17 July
    Purchase: One contract of September 390 series puts for 39p 'to open'
    Share price: 353p

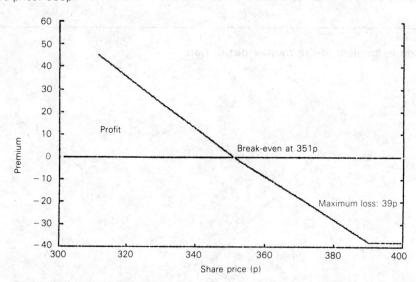

FIG. 3.2 Put option purchase: GKN Engineering − 17 July to 24 July.

Maximum loss: 39p per contract at striking price of 390p
Break-even: (390p − 39p (premium price) = 351p

CLOSING CONTRACT
    Date: 24 July
    Sale: One contract of September 390 series puts 'to close' for 61p
    Share price: 330p

Total premium received on sale of contract: 61p (intrinsic + timetable). Time value: intrinsic value = (390p − 330p) = 60p; time value left = 1p.

On 17 July the premiums (offer prices) were quoted as follows:

Option	Premium	Puts			Option	Premium	Puts		
		Sept	Dec	Mar			Sept	Dec	Mar
GKN 353*					GKN 330*				
17 July	300	3	4	—	24 July	300	4	6	—
	330	6	8	12		330	14	17	20
	360	16	19	21		360	31	35	38
	390	39	41	43		390	61	62	64

* Share price

PROFIT ON 24 JULY

Cost of opening contract:	39p	(Debit)
Received on closing contract:	61p	(Credit)
Net profit (before dealing expenses)	22p	(+ 56 per cent)

There is still some time value attached (1p), since this option was closed out before expiry date.

Worked examples: out-of-the-money puts options

An option which is currently out-of-the-money, has no intrinsic value. The only value attached to it is time value, which reflects the time period involved to expiry. Also, the amount by which the put is out-of-the-money together with the volatility of the stock is reflected in the time value. So, the deeper out-of-the-money the exercise price is, the cheaper the premium will be.

Example 1: GKN Engineering: use of out-of-the-money options

Option	Premium	Puts			Option	Premium	Puts		
		Sept	Dec	Mar			Sept	Dec	Mar
GKN 353*					GKN 330*				
17 July	300	3	4	—	24 July	300	4	6	—
	330	6	8	12		330	14	17	20
	360	16	19	21		360	31	35	38
	390	39	41	43		390	61	62	64

* Share price

The share price has fallen from 353p to 330p — a fall of approximately 6.5 per cent in just over a week. However, the option premiums have *risen* as shown below:

Out-of-the-money 300 Sept series has risen by 33 per cent (3p–4p);
Out-of-the-money 330 Sept series has risen by 133 per cent (6p–14p);
In-the-money 360 Sept series has risen by 94 per cent (16–31p);
In-the-money 390 Sept series has risen by 56 per cent (39p–61p).

In this example the out-of-the-money options, 330 Sept series, have shown the largest percentage increase: 133 per cent.

The 300 Sept series, which is also an out-of-the-money option, has not increased quite so much, since it is deeper out-of-the-money than the 330 Sept series and will consequently require a more dramatic fall in the share price to make the equivalent percentage gain in the option premium.

If the investor feels that the share price is going to decrease dramatically over a short period, e.g. bad final results are expected, then he should still think carefully before purchasing out-of-the-money options.

Let's now have a look at the risk/reward and break-even profiles for the 330 September series.

Break-even and risk/reward graphs for out-of-the-money puts

Example 1 (cont.): GKN September 330 series puts
See Fig. 3.3.

OPENING CONTRACT

  Date: 17 July
  Purchase: One contract of Sept 330 series puts 'to open' for 6p
  Share price: 353p

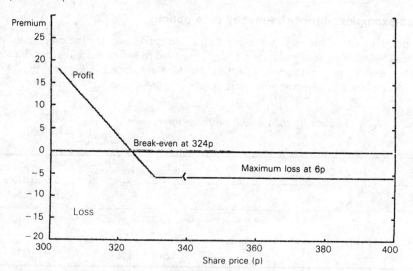

FIG. 3.3 Put option purchase: GKN Engineering – 17 July to 24 July at expiry.

  Maximum loss: 6p per contract at striking price of 330p
  Break-even: (330 − 6p) = 324p

CLOSING CONTRACT
  Date: 24 July
  Sale: On contract of Sept 330 series PUTS 'to close' for 14p

Share price: 330p
Total premium received on sale of contract: 14p ('at-the-money')

PROFIT ON 24 JULY

Cost of opening contract: 6p (Debit)
Received on closing contract: 14p (Credit)
Net profit (before dealing expenses): 8p (+133 per cent)

For a fall in the share price of 6.5 per cent, the investor has made a return on his investment of 133 per cent in just over a week.

Remember! Once you have 'purchased' a 'put' or a 'call' option to open a contract you should always inform your broker to 'close' the contract by 'selling to close' the appropriate option series.

EXPIRY OF OPTION CONTRACTS

The expiry date for each series is announced at the time of its initial listing, and dealings in an expiring series cease at 3.40 p.m. on the expiry date. Exercise notices are not accepted by LOCH after 6.00 p.m. on that date.

AUTOMATIC EXERCISE OF EXPIRY CONTRACTS

Market-makers

A reference price is set, based on the 3.40 p.m. price on the day of expiry, and all *but the nearest* in-the-money series, based on that reference price, will be automatically exercised. Where the reference price is exactly at-the-money, then that series will *not* be automatically exercised, but the next nearest in-the-money will be automatically exercised.

For example, if the underlying share price at 3.40 p.m. on the day of expiry is 361p, then the 360 call option series will not be automatically exercised, nor will the 390 put series – both series being the nearest in-the-money series. If the 3.40 p.m. price is exactly 360p, then neither the 360 call series nor the 360 put series will be exercised; but the 330 call series and the 390 put series will be automatically exercised.

Firm and client accounts

A reference price will be set based on the 3.40 p.m. price on the day preceding the expiry day. In-the-money series, based on the reference price, will be automatically exercised on expiry day with the following exceptions:

1. All in-the-money series which are within one per cent (rounded to the nearest full penny with 0.5p being rounded up) of the reference price.
2. The nearest in-the-money series. Where the nearest in-the-money was within one per cent then neither the nearest nor next nearest in-the-money will be exercised automatically.

USE OF PUT OPTIONS

Puts can be used for *protection* as well as investment. An investor anticipating that the stock market will decline in the near future may, instead of selling his stock, purchase a put option in the FT-SE Index. Any loss suffered by his portfolio from a decline in the market is then offset by the gain from the FT-SE put option.

For example, in July when the FT-SE Index stood at 1,667 you could have purchased a September 1,675 put option for the cost of 62p for contract (total cost for contract being £620). On 24 July the index stood at 1,547, a fall of 6.89 per cent: so, the put option purchased would have been worth a bid price of 115p on 24 July 1986. Therefore, you could have traded in the option at a profit 53p per contract, showing a return of 85 per cent on your original investment in three weeks!

Thus, by the use of traded options, you have avoided selling short on your stock whilst at the same time protecting your portfolio against the loss suffered from a down turn in the market. Perhaps your individual portfolio has not suffered and in this case you profit from your foresight.

Another example of using the FT-SE Index to purchase puts was on 1 October 1987 just before 'Black Monday'! Purchasing the October 2,400 puts at 58p (offered) with the market standing at just below this level and selling them on 22 October for 550p to give you a profit of 848 per cent in three weeks!

GENERAL RULES FOR PUT OPTION PURCHASES

The following are some general guidelines to help you in your purchases:

1. Don't buy puts unless the market is heavily overbought. (See Chapter four on Technical Analysis.) If the market is still firm, it is very difficult to make money out of a particular stock which appears to be overvalued. It is better to wait until the market is generally weaker; then attack the particular stock by the purchase of put options.

FAN FORMATIONS

EARLY WARNING SIGNALS FOR THE FANS !

The FTSE chart is still showing the classic fan formation. The longer term 'FAN' formation with support lines AB & AC and the smaller intermediary well developed fan formation at 1, 2, 3 & 4.

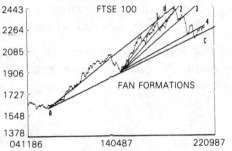

So what is a 'Fan Formation'? First of all, a fan formation is so called because it resembles the pattern of a fan opening out. It is basically a build up of support lines as is the case with the FTSE chart (or resistance lines) which are continuously being broken over a period of time and so the chart begins to look like a fan.

The fan formation gives the investor early warning signals of when to pull out of the market or a particular share. (The reverse fan tells you when to get back in).

The fan formation is drawn by taking the low point of the share/index and connecting this up with the next secondary low to form the first support line. When the Index breaks through this first line of support (line 1) it will then continue to fall until further support is found. The original low is then connected to the next low and a support line (line 2) is then drawn in and so on.

What the chart is trying to tell you is that if the Index breaks through the first support line at 1. Then this is a sign that the market could be due for a change downward so the amber light goes on and says "Watch out!". If the Index continues to fall through the second line of support (line 2) then the chart is saying "Yes, this is really the time to think of pulling out". If you had not pulled out or taken up put options by the time it penetrated line 4 then be it on your own shoulders!

The support lines often turn into resistance lines once the Index/Share has penetrated through the support line. This can be seen clearly in the chart at line 1 when the Index fell through its support line (line 1) which in turn then became the resistance line which it failed to penetrate.

'FAN FORMATIONS' are good early warning signals assisting you in the timing and informing you in which direction the market is likely to go.

Fundamentally the market is still very liquid with pending rights issues in the pipeline, second instalment of TSB and the forthcoming privatisation of BP. The reverse yield gap is still too wide and Wall St's recent increase in its discount rate to support the dollar was well timed with the Labour Day holiday on the Monday but has still had a negative effect with the Dow Jones falling 62 points at one stage. This must have a knock on effect with the UK!

Stick with the 2350 Calls that were sold at 16p last week and SELL 2350 Calls again at 10p.

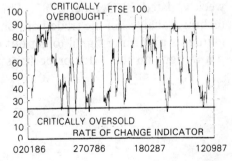

FIG. 3.4 Extract from *Traded Options Newsletter*, 28 October 1987.

2. When your profit target has been achieved, don't be afraid to close out your position.
3. It is better to purchase in-the-money or at-the-money put options, rather than out-of-the-money. If the investor is convinced that the share price of a stock is going to fall, then the rate of fall is likely to be less than for the equivalent call option, where, for example, bid situations can have a dramatic effect on the out-of-the-money call option.

Don't forget the fundamental difference between a 'put' option and a 'call' option: the purchaser of a 'put' option expects the underlying security to go down in price.

SUMMARY

'Put options' confer the right to *sell a stock*, at a specified price (exercise price) on or before a specified date (expiry date).

Put and call options in a particular stock will have the same expiry dates and, whenever a new call series is introduced, a companion put series with the same striking price will simultaneously be added.

Put options can be used for both protection and investment. If the investor feels that the market is temporarily overbought, instead of selling his shares he may look for some kind of protection against the anticipated decline in the market by buying put options to provide a hedge.

Another strategy involves writing call options. This strategy will be discussed in more detail in Chapter Five.

Before leaving this chapter on put options, let's look at some actual worked examples of put options in the market.

Figure 3.4 is an extract from the *Traded Options Newsletter*, which appears weekly, dated 28 October 1987. This example clearly demonstrates the use of technical analysis in the traded options market. Basically the 'fan' formation was giving us a warning signal to get out of the market, or alternatively to purchase put options on the index or perhaps write covered calls on existing stocks.

FOUR

PHILOSOPHY OF CHARTING AND TIMING IN THE TRADED OPTIONS MARKET

INTRODUCTION

Charting has been used in the UK for some time and is now widely accepted as a means of forecasting future moves in share prices and commodities. The aim of this chapter is to enable the investor not only to understand the mechanics of charting but also, more importantly, to interpret the various patterns that develop.

Charts have two immediate advantages. Firstly, they represent a picture of the historic share price movement and the mind is able to assimilate this information much more quickly than a list of tabulated figures. Secondly, any major change in the share price, whether upwards or downwards, will *immediately* be noticed.

So we have initially established that charts do have a use. However, some fundamentalists will totally disregard charts and prefer to look at PE ratios (see Glossary), earnings, expected results and other outside factors, such as strikes and expected government trade figures. What charts do is tell the investor when a share is cheap in relation to its previous performance, and at which point it is a good time to buy the share or, alternatively, to sell it.

Chartists maintain that patterns tend to repeat themselves over a period of time. So, when an investor is studying a chart for a particular share and sees a pattern emerging, similar to a previous pattern, then the odds are in favour of the same pattern emerging again.

One of the most important factors when buying and selling options is *timing*: even a good share option bought at the wrong time could lead to your downfall! So, what the private investor is looking for is an *aid* which can assist in the *timing* of buying and selling of options. Charts can do this.

An investor who tries to buy at the bottom and sell at the top must either be very lucky or very foolhardy. The old adage to 'buy low and to sell high' is, however, as valid now as it was in the past. But what we have to try and establish is what is high and what is low in any particular stock? Again, charts can assist you in determining whether an option/share is cheap or expensive compared to its previous performance.

When the investor is buying options he/she is trying to cut down the element of risk as much as possible. Charts do cut down the element of risk; but the investor must remember that they do not completely eliminate it. As you will see as you go through this chapter, technical analysis can help you to increase your profits and reduce your losses. But, it is important to remember that it is the *interpretation* of these charts that will count in the end.

Some chartists will totally disregard fundamentals, as some fundamentalists totally disregard charts. However, I feel that it is best to try and achieve the correct balance of both, depending on whether you are more of a chartist or more of a fundamentalist. Some chartists even lock themselves in a room without windows so that the weather conditions outside will not influence their judgment! Naturally, this is extreme and a degree of fundamentalism should be considered before taking a decision from your charts.

The fundamental approach is, '*Should* I buy/sell?', whereas the technical approach is, '*When* should I buy/sell?'.

The philosophy of technical analysis is based on the simple premise that any movement in a share's price is caused by an imbalance between buyers and sellers. Emotions are the main reason why buyers buy and sellers sell. Buyers suffer from emotions of greed, whilst sellers suffer from emotions of fear. It follows that successful investment depends on some understanding of psychology. Indeed, charts and indices, on which so many religiously rely, are really an application of this science to the interpretation of stock market trends: progressions from which reasonable assumptions may be drawn as to future behaviour. What they show, in fact, is that human nature does not change – that an ascension of optimism over pessimism, or the reverse, is likely, other things being equal, to be perpetuated into the future.

What happens is that the investor at large becomes so persuaded of the inevitability of an established trend, so seduced by success that at the peak of the 'bull' market, as in the trough of the 'bear', there is usually a plateau-ing phase when the market either shades off the top or stirs off the bottom, to move, as we say, 'sideways' for a time and within narrow bounds.

The explanation for plateau-ing is that, although the market is already reacting fundamentally to changing influences, the investor is obstinately buying against the trend or, conversely, jettisoning his shares on the least lift off the bottom. To this extent the market seldom plummets dramatically from its peak or bounds off its bottom, so that the underlying trends are deceptively contradicted.

The investor who employs a little psychology will appreciate that there are times when it pays to swim conveniently with the tide; as equally there are others when it pays (and often better) to go perversely counter to the popular trend. In the early stages of a recovery, join the bandwagon, and enjoy the propulsive power of the herd instinct as the popular appetite is whetted by easy profit.

Now let us underline these considerations. There are two truisms to remember: 'What goes up must come down'; and the equally contestable, 'One person's gain is another's loss.'

Note how easily the newcomer to the market is seduced by the apparent ease of profit-making: as he/she embarks on a steadily rising trend – and that is where the newcomer inevitably comes in – on the strength of one, possibly two, quick fortuitous 'tickles', he becomes convinced of the possession of the 'open Sesame' to an Aladdin's Cave in Throgmorton Street! *This is the first fatal mistake.*

The further fact is that every newcomer, whether outside investor or inside practitioner, is conditioned subconsciously by his beginnings – the market climate on which he first entered. If it was entered in times of slump, then you will look back apprehensively over your shoulder or if in the heady days of boom without apparent end, then perhaps you will reach instinctively for the stars with little or no caution.

So, there is a constant battle between buyers and sellers. If a company's performance increases dramatically but both buyers and sellers remain equal, then the share price will remain the same no matter how well the company continues to perform. Only when buyers outnumber sellers and vice versa will the share price move.

The emotional nature of the market is fundamental to determining how a share price moves, and the technical analyst will concentrate on charting these emotions and predicting the times when they will spill over to cause a reversal. A typical example is a share price which has been moving along at a steady pace. The investor finds the share too boring, so decides not to invest his money in it. All of sudden the share price takes off, and the investor feels that he has missed the boat. The fundamentals sound good, too, so he/she decides to wait until a level of fear sets in and the investors who bought early decide to sell. As the level of selling increases, so the share price takes a short downturn. When the level of selling matches the level of buying, then the share price will stop falling and eventually the investor may decide to buy. Now more buyers than sellers exist, so the share price starts to rise again. The price continues to rise. In a bull market the share price will not fall as low as the previous low, before buyers move in again. Eventually a typical trading pattern is established in chart form and one begins to see a zig-zag line sloping upwards (in a bull market) or downwards (in a bear market). See Fig. 4.1.

Each short term *peak* on the zig-zag line is called the *resistance* level which is the point where the supply of stock available is sufficient to satisfy the buyers' demand. Each *trough* on the zig-zag line is called the *support* level, where buyers begin to gain the ascendancy as the share begins to look increasingly cheap, and the demand for the stock equals the supply.

Never be confused between technical analysis and chartism. Technical

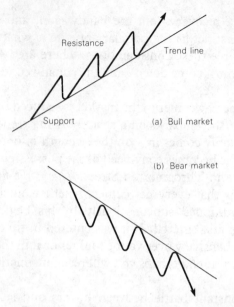

FIG. 4.1 Trading patterns of 'bull' and 'bear' markets.

analysis provides the guidance on the probability of share price movements in accordance with fundamental reasoning and is used to supplement, not to replace, fundamental principles of investment.

Chartism, on the other hand, provides positive 'buy' or 'sell' indicators, with no reference to probabilities of fundamentals whatsoever. Generally technical analysis covers all methods (other than using fundamental valuations) which will enable the investor to put current prices into perspective with a view to obtaining an indication as to whether a security's price is more likely to go up or down.

We will now look at some of the techniques and procedures of technical analysis. Remember timing is one of the most important, if not the most important, element when buying and selling options. Timing is about the wisdom – or unwisdom – of being involved. At rock bottom, one's ability to sell is dependent on another's ability – or willingness – to buy, and vice versa.

If timing is the touchstone of successful investment, then imagination is the background.

MECHANICS OF CHARTING

In the course of many years of stock market study, two distinct methods of analysis have arisen in answer to the questions of which stock to buy and when. The first of these methods is fundamental analysis and the second, technical analysis. The fundamental analyst's approach depends upon business statistics:

examining profit and loss statements, balance sheets, dividend records and company policies. He analyses turnover figures, managerial ability, competition and any business information given on the industry in question. After careful study, he arrives at an estimate of future business performance and, taking this into account, makes an evaluation of his stock. If it is currently selling below the rating he believes it should be on, he regards it as a 'buy'.

Technical analysis is concerned with none of these criteria. It refers to the study of price action – that is, the action of the market itself, rather than the goods and services in which the companies trade. The technical analyst looks at prices and price movements in the past and present. He records, usually in graphic form, and observes how share prices have moved historically and, by the additional use of certain confirmatory indicators, is able to forecast the probable future trend of the price. At any one moment, the price of a stock reflects the hopes and fears of thousands of potential buyers and sellers and represents the general opinion of investors as to its current worth. Many times the price action will defy the fundamental arguments behind it: in these circumstances, the technicians are in their element and can, perhaps, provide the only guide to trading decisions.

Although the techniques used in this method of analysis are applicable to any market situation where a price is regularly quoted and is extensively used – in commodities, options and foreign exchange dealings, for instance – for the purposes of illustration we shall concentrate on examples on the UK equity market.

The basis for the theory of the technical approach is that prices move in *trends*. These trends may be up, down or sideways; but sooner or later they will change. Profits can be made by following the up and down trends until they are reversed. The art of technical analysis is to spot when the turn has been made – the earlier the better.

Figure 4.2 shows a normal uptrend pattern. Suppose the price started off from

FIG. 4.2 Normal up trend pattern.

a major bottom and began to advance. The price moves up until it reaches a level (A) where our investor thinks it has gone far enough and sells at a profit. Following this, the price reacts (1) and he congratulates himself on his astuteness. However, the next day the price picks up again and pushes on to new higher levels (B). Our investor is not feeling so clever now – it was a better stock than he had given it credit for. He decides to buy it back if it should fall to the price he sold it for, which it duly does at (2). Now the upswing is gaining momentum, as both our investor and new purchasers move in and prices surge to new high ground (C) before again running into enough selling to stop the upward trend. This time, investors who sold at (B) buy back and the price continues to advance once again. A *trend* has developed and will continue until a reversal pattern appears.

There are two other factors to be observed here. Firstly, the price at which a share halts after a setback is called the *support* level – that is, the level at which sufficient *demand* for a stock appears to halt the down trend; while a *resistance* level is a price level at which sufficient *supply* of stock is forthcoming to stop an up trend.

The second observation is that it is evident that, if the various support levels are joined up, a *trendline* is formed (see Fig. 4.3). Trendlines are useful indicators: when the price breaks the trendline, it signals that the underlying characteristics for the upward momentum to resume have broken down and the trend may be changing direction. In bull markets the trendline is drawn joining the low points of price reactions, whilst in bear markets it is drawn joining the peaks of the rallies.

While trends can break down, the reaction may not always be as serious as it looks. Generally, there are three types of trend. The major trend, known as the 'primary' trend, can and usually does last for a number of years before a major reversal takes place. Within this primary trend are intermediate setbacks or rallies, which will last for some months: these are called 'secondary' trends. Finally the 'tertiary' trend will map out a short-term price movement and is followed more often by traders in the market than by longer-term investors, because of its short and less significant implications.

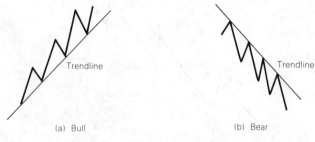

FIG. 4.3 Formation of trendlines.

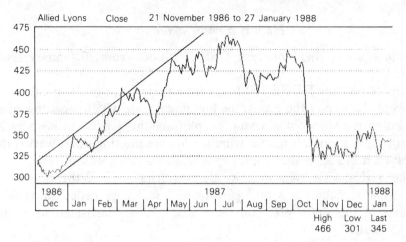

FIG. 4.4 Allied Lyons: up trend with upper resistance.

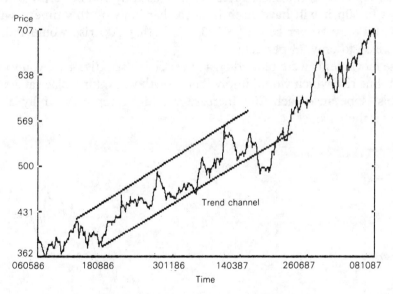

FIG. 4.5 BAT: a typical trend channel.

Figure 4.4 of Allied Lyons illustrates a typical uptrend cycle. An important point to remember is that the more points of *contact* there are on a trendline, the more significant is the implication for the share price when the trend is violated.

Sometimes lines can be drawn on the top and bottom of the price trend: when these lines are parallel the area between the extremities is known as a *trend channel*. Penetration of these return lines indicates an exhaustion move and characterises the terminal phase of a trend. Figure 4.5 showing British American Tobacco (BAT) also illustrates a typical 'trend channel'.

How is a chart made up?

Let's look at a line chart for the FT-SE 100 Index from 20 January 1986. See Fig. 4.6.

In order to plot the FT-SE 100 Index for a period of, say, 21 months, the first action would be to plot the *x* axis: the horizontal scale which measures *time*. It is important to remember when you are plotting the *x* axis, to keep each unit constant so that it doesn't matter whether you are plotting days, weeks, months or years: each block on the graph paper will measure a unit of time.

On the vertical scale, the *y* axis, we are measuring *price*. In this case it is better to use what is called a semi-logarithmetic' scale, in order to avoid large distortions in the share price on the *y* axis. Most chartists tend to use the 'semi-log' basis.

In order to illustrate better the concept of semi-log charts, assume a share price rises from 20p to 40p: the share price has increased by 100 per cent. If the price then rises to 60p it will have risen by a further 20p; by this time it will have increased by only 50 per cent ($\frac{20}{40} \times 100$). A further 20p rise would reduce the price increase to only 33 per cent.

If these movements were plotted on a linear chart (see Fig. 4.7), you would see a straight line rise which would imply that growth was taking place at a constant rate. This is because each 20p increase would be represented by a similar distance on the *y* axis.

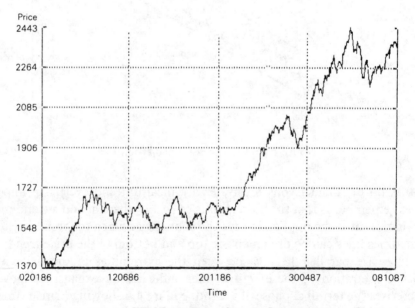

FIG. 4.6 FT-SE 100 Index from 20 January 1986.

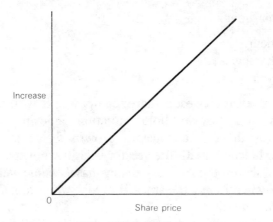

FIG. 4.7 **Linear chart.**

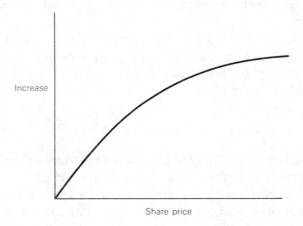

FIG. 4.8 Semi-logarithmic representation of a constant 20p share price.

The same chart plotted on a semi-logarithmetic scale would show a different picture. Instead, the rise in the price curve would gradually tail off as the price increased, which would more accurately depict the fact that growth in real terms was slowing down (see Fig. 4.8).

FUNDAMENTALISTS VERSUS CHARTISTS

Fundamentalists dismiss chart patterns and trends. They prefer to rely on a company's performance and its expected results, PE ratios, or even external factors – such as takeover situations or government action which might affect the share price movement. Fundamentalists, however, tend to overlook three important considerations:

1. Market sentiment.
1. Investor psychology.
3. The market cycle.

The fundamentalist examines each share, comparing it with its intrinsic value, and usually buys on a 'buy-and-hold' situation, ignoring the importance of timing. As long as there is a constant growth factor in the market, this philosophy is fine; however, with the greater volatility now persisting within the market – and in shares themselves, *timing* has become very important i.e. knowing not only when to *buy* the stock, but also when to *sell* it. This is where *charts* can assist the investor.

As mentioned earlier, any serious investor should not totally disregard charts or fundamentals: charts are often disregarded merely because the investor doesn't understand, sticking instead to the method of fundamentals which has been used for many years.

With the increasing demand for computerisation and computerised software on technical analysis (see Chapter Ten), more and more of the larger institutions are now employing highly paid staff as market analysts to report on the technical analysis of shares or commodities.

Summary

Fundamental analysis is the study of the trading performance and prospects of a company. Fundamental analysts will study the trading history of a company, evaluate its immediate and future prospects and then make a decision as to whether the share price is under- or overvalued, and buy and sell accordingly.

Technical analysis takes into account neither the financial health nor the prospects of a company, and looks purely at the action of the share price itself and the market in general. It attempts to discern a pattern or trend from past share-price movements and then predicts how that pattern will evolve in the short or long term.

The philosophy of technical analysis is based on the simple premise that any movement in a share's price is caused by an imbalance between buyers and sellers.

TRENDS

We will now study trends in more detail. Share prices tend to move in trends over a period of time. A trend is a reliable and steady pattern that can give the

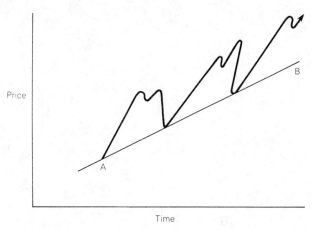

FIG. 4.9 Chart up trend.

investor a certain amount of confidence in the trend continuing. Once the investor notices that a trend has been established, it is best to act on this: to buy the share as soon as possible and not sell it until the trend has been broken. Never try and force a trend: if the trend doesn't exist, look for other patterns or indicators that may assist you in the timing of your investment.

There are two types of trends: up trends and down trends.

Up trends

In order to construct an 'up' trend, it is necessary to connect the *lower* points of the share price during its rise. In order for the trend line to be confirmed, a contact of three points is usually considered to be valid. The longer the trendline has been in force, the more validity it will have.

In Fig. 4.9 we have connected the three low points of the share price and formed an up trend A–B. This up trend is the *support* level for the share price. Each time the share price hits this level it finds support (i.e. more buyers than sellers), and continues to rise to higher ground.

Now let's look at some up trends in the real market.

Marks & Spencer

In Fig. 4.10 for M & S, we have the share price rising from 212p at point A to 220p at point B, falling back again to 216p at point C, then rising again.

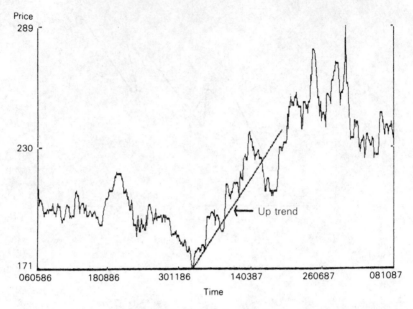

FIG. 4.10 Marks & Spencer: up trend.

Imperial Chemical Industries (ICI)

Figure 4.11 also confirms the up trend formation.

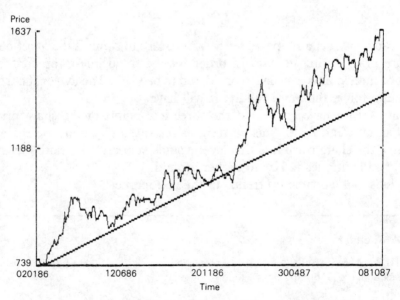

FIG. 4.11 ICI: up trend.

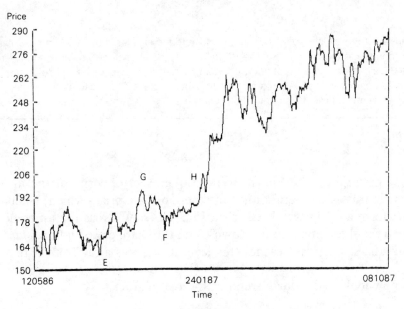

FIG. 4.12 Cadbury: primary up trend.

Cadbury

With the next example, Cadbury (Fig. 4.12), take out a ruler and pencil and plot the up-trend yourself. Join the major low at point E to the secondary low at point F. The secondary low is the first major correction the share price suffers after minor interruptions. The up trend continues because the next high at point H is above the previous high at point G; so we now know when we have an up trend in the making.

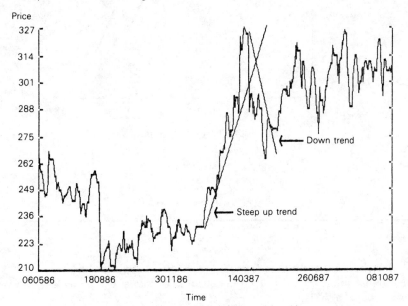

FIG. 4.13 Boots: sharp uptrend followed by down trend.

Boots

If there are a number of low points connected close together, then the share is more volatile and a sudden change in the direction of the trendline is to be expected. Similarly, a very steep up trend will usually result in a correction, and in some cases may even result in a down trend being formed. A steep up trend formation often occurs when there is a 'bid' situation, as was the case with Boots recently. Fig. 4.13 clearly illustrates the steep up trend followed by a down trend.

Down trends

As the name implies, the 'down' trend is the exact opposite of the up trend. However, in this case we are connecting the top share prices which, when joined together, form a down trend AB. (See Fig. 4.14.) Whereas the up trend gives support to the share price, in the down trend the share price finds *resistance*, and each time the share price reaches this level it bounces away from it to a lower level.

Let's now look at the down trend in the real market.

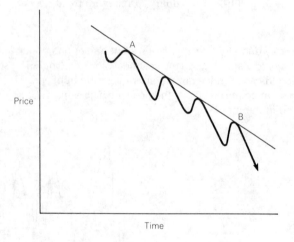

FIG. 4.14 Chart down trend.

Jaguar

In Fig. 4.15 we have the share price falling from a high of 630p at point A to 547p at point B. During the formation of this down trend the share price rallies, but continuously fails to rise above its previous major high.

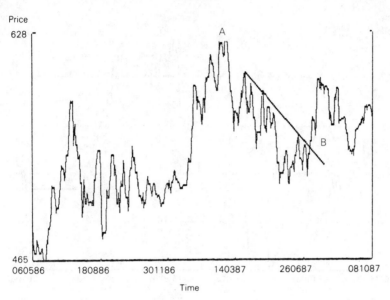

FIG. 4.15 Jaguar: down trend.

Penetration of trendlines

Eventually these trendlines which we have been discussing will be broken, either because the share price is too cheap and there are more buyers than sellers or because the share price becomes too expensive and there are more sellers than buyers.

If the share price penetrates upwards through the resistance level as in a down trend, or down through the support level as in an up trend by 3 per cent or more from the breakthrough point, then the trend can be considered to be broken, and a 'sell' or 'buy' signal given accordingly. Most chartists believe that the penetration must break through by at least 3 per cent before the trendline can be considered to be broken, and a *sell* or *buy* signal is given. (For the more cautious investor, some chartists use a 5 per cent breakthrough point for the appropriate buy/sell signal.)

British Aerospace

Figure 4.16 shows an example of the penetration of a down trend. The buy signal was given at point B when the down trend was broken and eventually the share price continued to rise fairly dramatically.

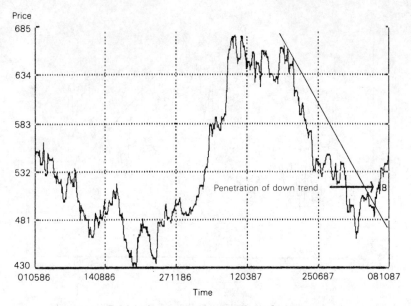

FIG. 4.16 British Aerospace: penetration of a down trend.

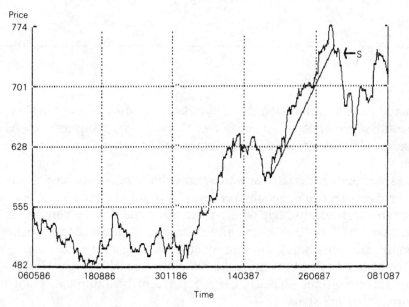

FIG. 4.17 P&O Shipping: penetration of an up trend.

P&O Shipping

Figure 4.17 shows an example of the penetration of an up trend. The sell signal was given at point S when the up trend was broken and the share price then continued to fall.

By observing these trends we have noticed that the share price tends to bounce up and down between two levels. When a share price finds support (i.e. more buyers than sellers), this level is established and the share price ceases to fall any further; in fact it then starts to rise until it reaches a level at which there is sufficient supply of the stock to halt an advance, and the share price finds resistance.

These two levels – *support* and *resistance* – are very important to the chartist in the interpretation of future price movements. Both are interchangeable and, if a share price pushes through a resistance level, this can then become the share's new support level.

Tesco

Figure 4.18 shows an example of a support level becoming the resistance level. Tesco's share price finds resistance at the level A–B; this then turns into a support line from B to C.

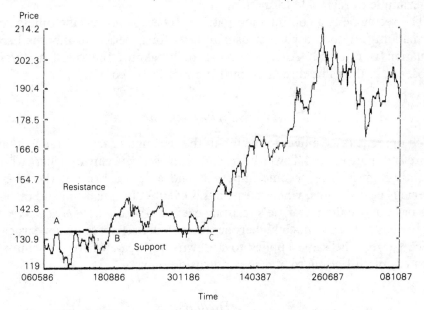

FIG. 4.18 Tesco: resistance level becoming support level.

Rectangles

A rectangular pattern develops from the share price continually bouncing off its support level, and then away from its resistance level back to the support level. Eventually a pattern shaped like a rectangle is formed. In this formation the

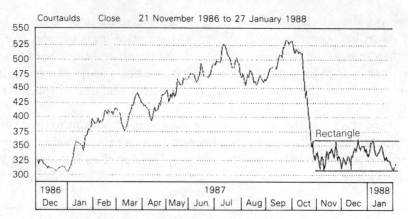

FIG. 4.19 Courtaulds: example of rectangle formation.

resistance and support levels must be parallel to each other. Figure 4.19 shows an example of rectangle formation.

The rectangle is a continuation pattern. There is no specific timescale for its formation, but such a pattern usually lasts for a period of months before the situation is resolved. After a premature breakout, the trend almost always proceeds in the same direction until the real break comes.

Supply vacuum

Each time the price moves to the top of the rectangular trading range it takes out more and more sellers. Towards the end of the sequence many sellers who want a slightly higher price become impatient and accept a price at the level of the previous peaks. Thus, when the selling is eventually exhausted and buyers push the price above the rectangle's resistance levels, there is a *supply vacuum* and the jobber has to bid up much higher for stock before sellers again appear, causing a price surge. The same applies to a downside break where a vacuum is also created, often leading to a vicious downside move.

Breakouts

As explained above, a breakout will occur from the rectangle either way. A clue to the breakout is often given by the share price either moving away from the support line, and eventually breaking upwards out of the rectangle, or alternatively moving away from the resistance line and eventually breaking downwards (see Fig. 4.20).

When the share price does break out of the rectangle the move is likely to equal the height of the pattern. So, the chartist is able from these patterns to predict the likely move with some confidence.

(a) Breakout upwards   (b) Breakout downwards

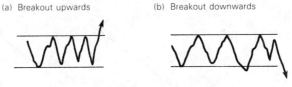

FIG. 4.20 Breakout patterns.

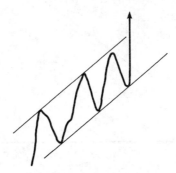

FIG. 4.21 Up trend channel.

Sloping rectangle formations

Rectangles do not necessarily have to be upright: they can slope either upwards or downwards. There are two important points to remember:

1. The lines of support and resistance must be parallel.
2. The longer the rectangle takes to form, the more it has to reverse.

Trend channels

Again, these patterns consist of two parallel lines, slanting upwards for an uptrend channel, with the price moving between the lower support line, whilst the upper parallel line acts as a resistance line. (See Fig. 4.21).

Trend channels can be a very good aid for the chartist in the traded options market. When the share bounces off its lower parallel support line, step in then and buy call options. As the share reaches the upper parallel resistance line, close the call options and buy puts. The same principle applies in reverse to a downtrend channel.

Let's have a look at a few examples of trend channels in the market.

Trusthouse Forte

See Fig. 4.22 for an example of an up trend channel.

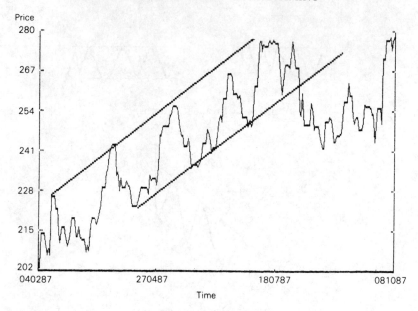

FIG. 4.22 Trusthouse Forte: up trend channel.

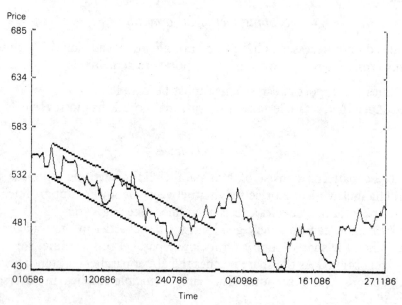

FIG. 4.23 British Aerospace: down trend channel.

British Aerospace

See Fig. 4.23 for an example of a down trend channel.

Penetration of the lower parallel line is a selling signal, since a further fall in the share price can be expected. Again, it is best to wait for at least 3 per cent penetration before acting.

In an uptrend channel you *buy* when the share price bounces off the support line.

In a downtrend channel you *sell* when the share price bounces off the resistance level.

Triangles

Basically, there are five types of triangles:

1. Symmetrical.
2. Ascending.
3. Descending.
4. Inverted.
5. Wedge.

Symmetrical triangle
Figure 4.24 shows that each successive up move ends *below* the previous one and each successive down move ends *above* the previous one. Eventually a breakout will occur from the triangular formation, upwards or downwards, and ideally two-thirds along the way of the triangle formation. See also Fig. 4.25 for a 'real-life' example.

Ascending triangle
As we can see in Fig. 4.26, the resistance line is horizontal. Again, a breakout should ideally occur two-thirds across the triangle formation. The larger the pattern, the more significant the break. See also Fig. 4.27 for a 'real-life' example.

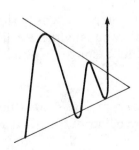

FIG. 4.24 Symmetrical triangle.

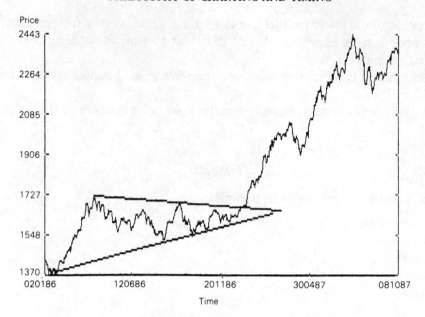

FIG. 4.25 FT-SE 100: symmetrical triangle.

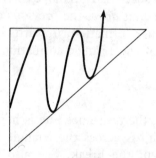

FIG. 4.26 Ascending triangle.

Descending triangle
As you can see in Fig. 4.28, the support line is horizontal. Demand is falling but supply remains the same, and eventually there will be a fall in the share price. See also Fig. 4.29 as a 'real-life' example.

Inverted triangle
The triangular formation shown in Fig. 4.30 is not very reliable! But like all triangular formations the more points of contact that exist, the more reliable the pattern.

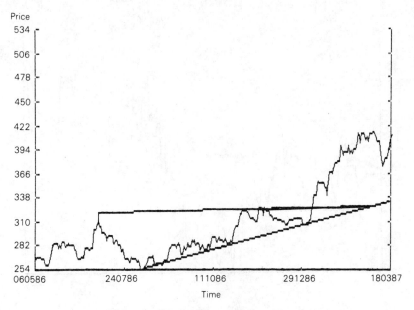

FIG. 4.27 Courtaulds: ascending triangle.

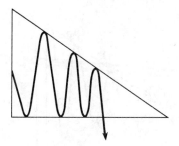

FIG. 4.28 Descending triangle.

Wedges

In this formation there are two trend lines drawing together and sloping in the same direction to form a *wedge*. A wedge pattern normally marks an imminent *reversal* of the share price to breakout in the opposite direction. Wedge formations normally have more points of contact than typical triangular formations. They will generally appear with a falling apex in the up trend and a rising apex in the down trend.

Racal has been used as an example of a wedge formation. The wedge is quite clear with both lines pointing markedly downwards. (See Fig. 4.31.) Both

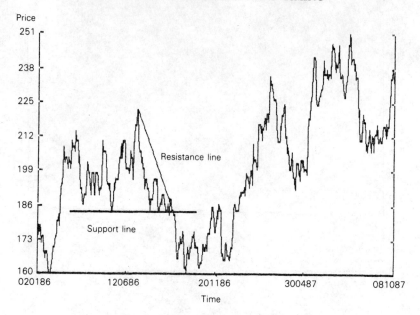

FIG. 4.29 GEC: descending triangle.

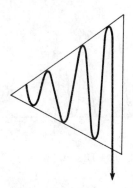

FIG. 4.30 Inverted triangle.

buyers and sellers are in competition with each other. Eventually the buyers win and Racal's share price takes off on the upside. As with triangles, you want the breakout to occur before its apex.

MOVING AVERAGES

Timing: the difference between investment success and failure

Ask yourself: would your analysis warn you of a down trend in time to get out of

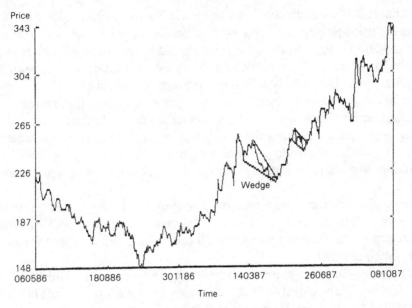

FIG. 4.31 Racal: wedge formation.

the market? If the answer is no, then you should perhaps take a look at one of the oldest and most successful indicators: the *moving average*.

If you have already learned about moving averages, but have classed them with all those other charting techniques, then reconsider their particular usefulness. If you are not familiar with this method, then you should follow the following steps:

1. Obtain the last 25 price pages from your daily newspaper. This should give you five weeks of daily price fixings. If you have not kept these copies, back issues will be available from the paper's head office. Number these pages from one to 25, with one as the oldest and 25 as the most recent.

2. Now take the 20 oldest price pages (numbers 1 to 20) and, choosing one share which interests you, make a list of its closing prices in date order.

3. Add all these prices together and divide them by 20 – in other words, work out what the average price has been over days 1 to 20. Write this average down next to day 20's price in our list.

4. Now write down the price for day 21 below day 20's price and cross out day 1's price so that you still have 20 prices in your list. Now, add them up and divide by 20, so giving a new or 'moving' average. Again, cross off day 2, add in day 22 and re-calculate your moving average. Go on until you reach day 25 (today's price).

5. The next step is to get a piece of ordinary graph paper. Label the vertical side 'Price in pence' and the horizontal side 'Days'. Consider the list of prices that

you have written down and choose a scale for the vertical axis to accommodate the price range which you have and at the same time leave a little spare at the top and bottom, in case the price should move outside its current range. Along the horizontal axis mark off one day for each small square, beginning at day 20 – you do not have a moving average before that.

6. You are now ready to plot your daily prices and moving average. In the column representing day 20 (which should be on the extreme left-hand side of your graph page), make a dot for the price and the moving average of that day. If you have chosen a share which has been falling, you will almost certainly find that the moving average dot is above the daily price, and vice versa.

   Now plot the remaining four days (numbers 21–25), so that you end up with two dots in each of the five left-hand columns. Join all the dots representing the moving average with one colour and all those for the daily price with another.

7. Each day re-calculate your moving average, adding on the latest price fixing and leaving off the oldest so that you always get the average of the last 20 days' prices, and plot it together with the daily price on your chart.

Example

Let us consider an imaginary company, ABC PLC. See Table 4.1.

TABLE 4.1 ABC PLC: ruling prices.

Day	Price (p)	Moving average
1	200	
2	190	
3	192	
4	185	
5	180	
6	185	
7	177	
8	170	
9	172	
10	167	
11	160	
12	163	
13	167	
14	160	
15	155	
16	152	
17	155	
18	160	
19	152	
20	140	169
21	142	166
22	138	163
23	135	161
24	137	158
25	130	156

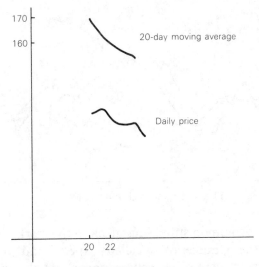

FIG. 4.32 ABC PLC: ruling prices.

The prices and their 20-day moving average would be charted as shown in Fig. 4.32.

A moving average simply smoothes the erratic daily fluctuations of a share's price and shows only the main trends. Whenever the daily price graph cuts down through the moving average, you should regard this as a selling signal, and whenever the daily price cuts back up this is your buy signal. Consider Fig. 4.33 together with its 10-week moving average.

The cumulative effect over the period shown of buying and selling at the points indicated would have been an increase of approximately 87 per cent on your investment, before dealing costs.

Your 20-day moving average is actually quite sensitive and may indicate more transactions than you would like. If this is the case, simply take a longer moving average i.e. 30 days or more. The longer your moving average, the fewer signals you will have, but the fewer profit opportunities will open to you.

Sideways-moving market

The time when the moving average does not work is in a sideways market. In other words, when your share's price stays in a narrow band for a long period you will find that your buy and sell signals are frequent, without much profit to cover your dealing costs. It is suggested that when you find that you have made transactions in fairly rapid succession you should get out of the shares and put your money elsewhere, until a clear break down or up is established. If this break is down, then you have lost nothing as you are already out of the market.

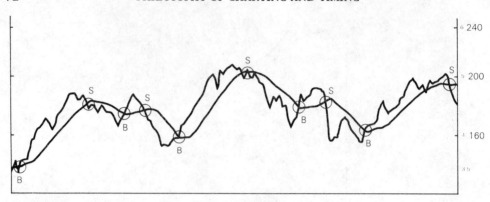

FIG. 4.33 Ten-week moving average.

Probably the most common stumbling block in the market is subjectivity. We are all swayed by the opinions of so-called 'experts' and, more than that, we naturally feel disappointment when we lose money, and elation when we make it. These subjective influences should never be allowed to interfere with the cold objective facts in your charts. When the daily price breaks down through the moving average, don't listen to stories about the IMF or the US dollar: make sure you have a good reason not to sell your shares!

Moving averages in practice

As suggested earlier, a 20-day moving average is a useful gauge, but you may find this too short and too sensitive. You would probably do better to use a 50-day moving average to give stronger signals.

It is not necessary to draw a graph to derive your signals. All you need do is see whether the moving average is higher or lower than the day's price. If it is higher, then your share is in a down trend and vice versa. When it changes from being higher to being lower this is a buy signal, and vice versa.

Finally, have you asked yourself why it is that the moving average technique works? To answer this question you should consider whether share prices move in an entirely random fashion – because if they do, it would not be possible to predict them. Clearly they don't, and the reason for this lies in the nature of the human animal: if you have a share which is trading at 20p, you will not accept 5p for it today. You might accept 18p, and tomorrow 16p, and the day after 14p, but you will not accept 5p today. This is because you, like all people, cannot adjust your frame of values downwards that quickly. So that, even though your share may eventually reach 5p, it will take time for this to happen as the investing public gradually adjusts its perception of the share's value. This slowness gives you time to get out of the share – its daily price will cut downwards through its moving average, to give you a sell signal.

Remember! To the extent that something is not random, it is predictable. It is simply a matter of finding a mathematical tool to predict a pattern. The moving average is a crude but effective method for taking advantage of humanity's inability quickly to adjust its frame of values up and down!

Table 4.2 shows the closing share prices for Glaxo during late June and July 1987, together with the 20-day, 50-day and 200-day moving averages.

TABLE 4.2 Glaxo: moving average

Date	Price	Average: 20-day	Average: 50-day	Average: 200-day
9 6 87	1750.00	1626.90	1538.31	1341.11
10 6 87	1762.00	1636.25	1544.49	1345.37
11 6 87	1725.00	1643.15	1549.74	1349.45
12 6 87	1750.00	1651.30	1555.74	1353.63
13 6 87	1750.00	1659.45	1562.00	1357.90
14 6 87	1750.00	1667.60	1568.26	1362.13
15 6 87	1750.00	1675.45	1574.52	1366.31
16 6 87	1750.00	1683.60	1581.40	1370.46
17 6 87	1787.00	1694.20	1588.64	1374.80
18 6 87	1725.00	1700.15	1594.28	1378.82
19 6 87	1675.00	1703.60	1599.16	1382.65
20 6 87	1675.00	1707.05	1604.04	1386.42
21 6 87	1675.00	1708.95	1608.92	1390.19
22 6 87	1650.00	1710.20	1613.30	1393.91
23 6 87	1662.00	1711.75	1617.92	1397.71
24 6 87	1687.00	1713.00	1623.16	1401.63
25 6 87	1737.00	1716.10	1629.40	1405.81
26 6 87	1731.00	1718.90	1635.40	1409.85
27 6 87	1731.00	1721.70	1640.52	1413.78
28 6 87	1731.00	1722.65	1645.64	1417.69
29 6 87	1687.00	1719.50	1649.88	1421.30
30 6 87	1662.00	1714.50	1652.88	1424.85
1 7 87	1643.00	1710.40	1655.62	1428.31
2 7 87	1668.00	1706.30	1657.98	1431.89
3 7 87	1675.00	1702.55	1659.98	1435.38
4 7 87	1675.00	1698.80	1661.98	1438.71
5 7 87	1675.00	1695.05	1664.24	1441.95
6 7 87	1687.00	1691.90	1666.74	1445.14
7 7 87	1737.00	1689.40	1670.24	1448.57
8 7 87	1775.00	1691.90	1674.00	1452.20
9 7 87	1762.00	1696.25	1677.74	1455.76
10 7 87	1762.00	1700.60	1681.48	1459.34
11 7 87	1762.00	1704.95	1684.98	1462.93
12 7 87	1762.00	1710.55	1688.48	1466.51
13 7 87	1750.00	1714.95	1691.74	1470.04
14 7 87	1775.00	1719.35	1695.50	1473.69
15 7 87	1837.00	1724.35	1700.38	1477.62
16 7 87	1843.00	1729.95	1705.50	1481.59
17 7 87	1837.00	1735.25	1710.74	1485.52
18 7 87	1837.00	1740.55	1715.36	1489.46
19 7 87	1837.00	1748.05	1719.98	1493.39
20 7 87	1812.00	1755.55	1724.10	1497.20
21 7 87	1793.00	1763.05	1727.22	1500.92
22 7 87	1775.00	1768.40	1730.22	1504.54
23 7 87	1750.00	1772.15	1732.60	1508.04
24 7 87	1762.00	1776.50	1734.60	1511.60
25 7 87	1762.00	1780.85	1736.34	1514.95
26 7 87	1762.00	1784.60	1738.08	1518.01

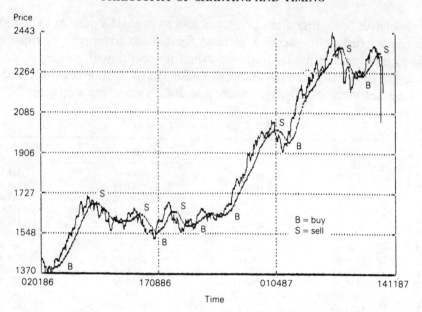

FIG. 4.34 FT-SE 100: 25-day moving average – with buy and sell signals.

As with most chart indicators, the important element with moving averages is to select the right timespans which not only fit best the share but also your type of investment. In the traded options market, chartists often look for shorter-term moving averages, or a combination of both, to give buy and sell signals. For instance, the FT-SE 100 Index responds particularly well to the 25-day moving average.

In the chart for FT-SE 100 (Fig. 4.34), the 25-day moving average gave six buy signals over a period of 23 months and six sell signals over the same period. If you had used a 10-day moving average, as indicated in Fig. 4.35, you would have been in and out of the index much more often.

By using the software computerisation now available (see Chapter Ten) the investor can quite easily find out the 'best fit' moving average unique to his particular share.

The following charts for Barclays (Figs. 4.36–4.43) show the 5-day, 10-day, 20-day, 25-day, 30-day, 50-day, 200-day and 13-week moving averages, with the buy points highlighted. In this case, the 50-day moving average gave the investor the best buying and selling points.

Lagged moving averages

Lagged moving averages are now also commonly used. Here more weighting is given to the latest entry and the lowest weighting to the most distant entry.

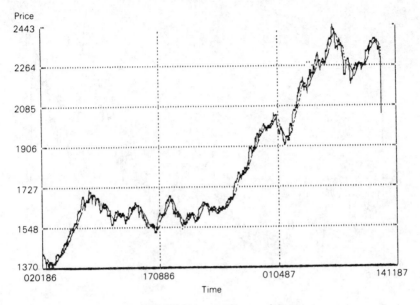

FIG. 4.35 FT-SE 100: ten-day moving average.

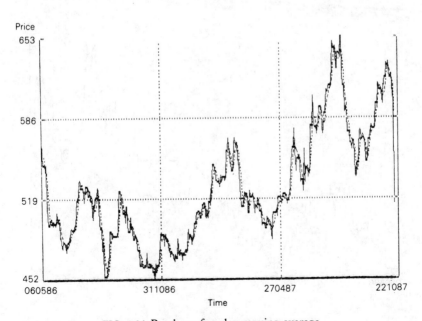

FIG. 4.36 Barclays: five-day moving average.

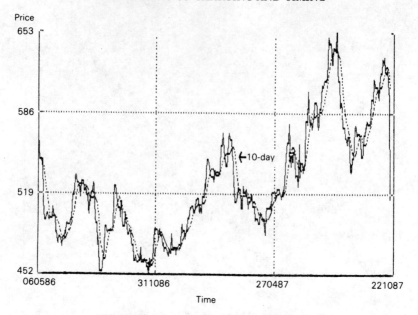

FIG. 4.37 Barclays: 10-day moving average.

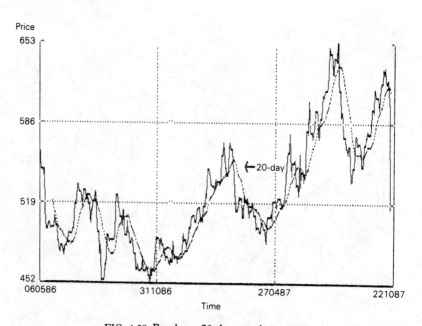

FIG. 4.38 Barclays: 20-day moving average.

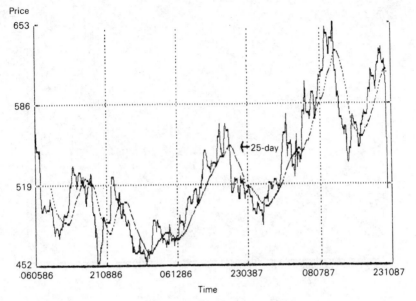

FIG. 4.39 Barclays: 25-day moving average.

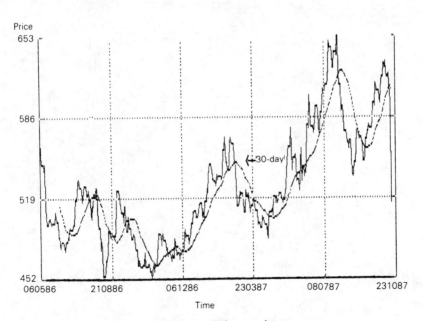

FIG. 4.40 Barclays: 30-day moving average.

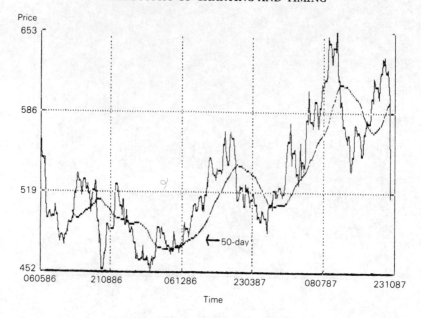

FIG. 4.41 Barclays: 50-day moving average.

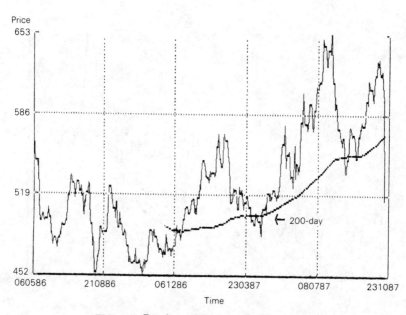

FIG. 4.42 Barclays: 200-day moving average.

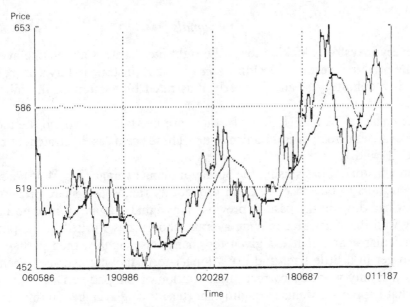

FIG. 4.43 Barclays: 13-week moving average.

However, over a longer period such as a 200-day moving average, the lagged effect does not play such an important role.

In a weighted five-day moving average, for example, the figure for day one is multiplied by one, the figure for day two is multiplied by two, the figure for day three is multiplied by three, etc. These figures are then added together to form a weighted total of 85, compared with the simple total of 30. See Table 4.3.

On day six, the simple total of 30 is deducted from the weighted total of 85 and the new weighted figure of 35 (5×7) is added ($85 - 30 + 35 = 90$). This is the new weighted total and, when divided by 15, becomes the second moving average plot.

TABLE 4.3 Weighted five-day moving average.

Day	Price	Simple	Weighted	Weighted total	Weighted moving average
1	6		$6 \times 1 = 6$		
2	7		$7 \times 2 = 14$		
3	8		$8 \times 3 = 24$		
4	4		$4 \times 4 = 16$		
5	5	30	$5 \times 5 = 25$	85	5.7
6	7	31	35	90	6.0
7	8	32	40	99	6.6

Buy signals

What every investor is looking for is the right *buy* signal. Can moving averages assist the private investor in deciding *when* is the right time to buy a share? The answer is a definite yes, and is clearly illustrated by examining the following charts.

In the chart for M & S (Fig. 4.44), there are five points at which the moving average changes direction from down to up. These occur, as illustrated, at points A, B, C, D and E.

So, on a historical basis using the 30-day moving average (Fig. 4.45), a signal was given to us to buy M & S. In all probability the M & S share price would rise, as it had done in the past on previous *buy* signals. Again, it is important to see how well the particular moving average chosen has worked in the past for that particular share. If it has given too many false signals, then perhaps it is better to get in a little later and use a longer-term moving average. Technical analysis will only work by correct interpretation of the patterns.

So, what happens if we use a slightly shorter moving average? In this case the moving average went many more times from down to up, confirming that the shorter moving average is more sensitive and can quite often give false signals.

By analysing the different moving averages, we can see that in the majority of cases the 50-day moving average has given a good *buy* signal and has led to good percentage profits. (Traded options investors often use 20-day or the Fibonacci numbers 4, 9, and 18.)

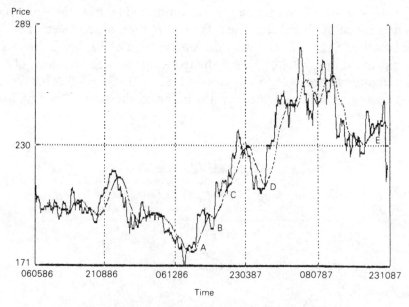

FIG. 4.44 Marks & Spencer: 20-day moving average.

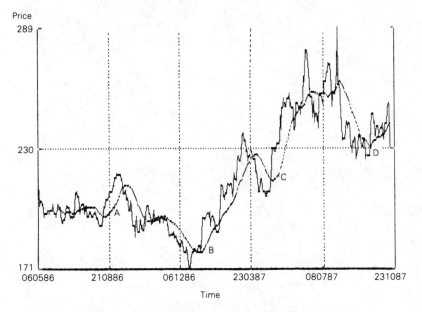

FIG. 4.45 Marks & Spencer: 30-day moving average.

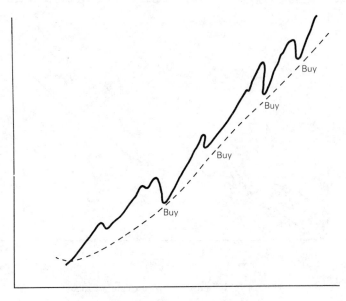

FIG. 4.46 Buy signals I.

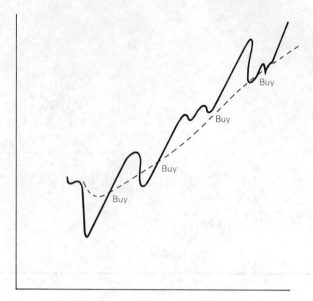

FIG. 4.47 Buy signals II.

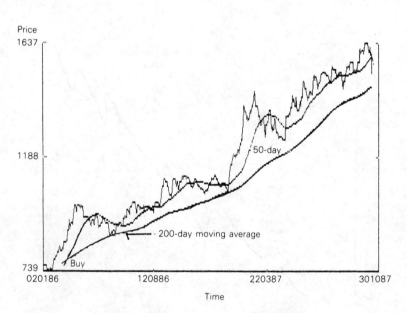

FIG. 4.48 ICI: use of two moving averages.

Again, whether you are a short-term or a longer-term investor will affect your decision as to which moving average to select.

The following is a list of buy signals. Up until now we have been talking about buy signals when the share price moves up through its moving average. However, there are two other important buy signals that should be recognised, points 2 and 3 below. All three are bullish indicators.

1. When the share price is moving up through its moving average, which itself is rising (as previously discussed).
2. When the share price moves down towards its moving average and then bounces off it.
3. When the share price temporarily falls through its moving average, which is still rising, and then bounces back through it.

See Figs. 4.46 and 4.47.

Combinations of moving averages: Golden crosses and dead crosses

The simple use of the long-term moving average by itself (e.g. 200-day), almost gives a rather late signal. In this instance, most chartists use two moving averages together, one often being 25 per cent of the other (e.g. 200-day and 50-day). See Fig. 4.48.

When both moving averages *cross* and *both* point upwards in the same direction then this is a strong *buy* indicator and is known as a *golden cross*. But beware when both moving averages draw towards each other but don't cross: this is usually a bearish indicator. Wait for the signal before acting. If both moving averages cross and one is pointing upwards whilst the other is pointing downwards, then this is not a golden cross. Act when the moving averages cross, but *only* when they are *both* pointing in the same direction.

A *dead cross* is exactly the opposite of a golden cross and action can be taken when both averages are pointing down and the shorter average cuts down through the longer one.

Examples

The following charts (Figs. 4.49 and 4.50) show how the golden cross and dead cross can be seen to work in the market. With Allied Lyons the golden cross is shown at points A using the 10-day and 20-day moving averages. With British Telecom a *sell* indicator was giving at point B: the classic dead cross formation also confirmed a *sell* indicator when the 10-day moving average crossed down through the 20-day moving average, which itself was moving down. The dead cross is at point B.

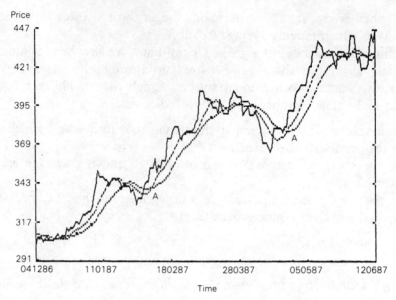

FIG. 4.49 Allied Lyons: a golden cross.

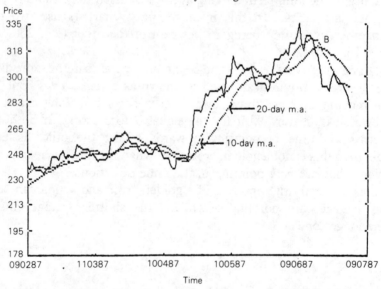

FIG. 4.50 BT: a dead cross.

Sell signals

Sell signals work in exactly the same way as buy signals with moving averages, but in reverse. Selling is often indicated by the moving average flattening out and then declining from up to down, the share price penetrating down through its moving average.

Example

Again, using a worked example in the market, let's look at Midland's share price and see how the 20-day (Fig. 4.51) and 50-day (Fig. 4.52) moving averages help the investor to sell his shares and still reap some good profits.

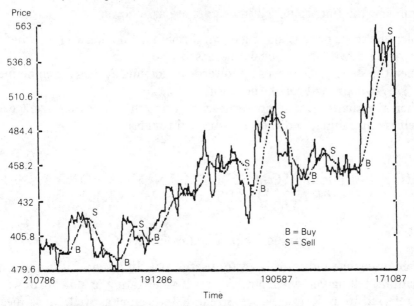

FIG. 4.51 Midland Bank: 20-day moving average – with buy and sell signals.

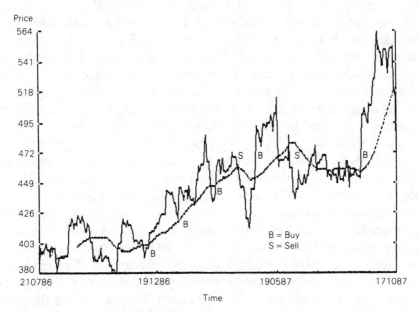

FIG. 4.52 Midland Bank: 50-day moving average – with buy and sell signals.

So again, using the historical basis (the 50-day moving average for Midland), a signal was given telling us to sell the shares. In all probability Midland's share price would still continue to fall. Again, you can practise using Midland's share price and different moving averages to find the best fit.

In summary, the important sell indicators are as follows:

1. When the share price is moving down through its moving average which itself is moving down (as previously discussed).
2. When the share price moves up towards its moving average, then bounces off it. This is a strong bearish indicator.
3. When the share price temporarily rises through its moving average which itself is still falling, and then falls back through it.

SHORT-TERM MOMENTUM INDICATORS IN THE TRADED OPTIONS MARKET

Rate of change indicator (ROC)

The rate of change indicator is a very useful tool. In essence, it is a measure of momentum, telling you when a move is still accelerating or slowing down. (It is often referred to as RSI (Relative Strength Indicator) as well.) It is measured between zero and 100; when the indicator is below 25 the underlying stock is said to be 'oversold' and when the ROC is above 75 it is said to be 'overbought'. In the example of Cable and Wireless (Fig. 4.53), the chart pattern of the ROC will highlight overbought and oversold positions. The fact that the stock is overbought or oversold is not in itself a reason to take action. It is only when the ROC begins to move *out* of these critical areas that the signal to buy or sell is given. In the example of Cable and Wireless, the sell indicators are highlighted at point B. By drawing a line directly to the corresponding share price below the ROC chart, you can see that these indicators worked very well.

Similarly with M & S (Fig. 4.54), the underlying share price has been overlayed on M & S's ROC chart to illustrate the use of the buy and sell indicators. A number of students have asked how to work out the ROC indicator manually and Table 4.4 illustrates the example with Cable and Wireless. However, with all the technical analysis aids it is very important to interpret the indicators quickly and not to spend too many laborious hours working out your moving averages, point and figure charts and ROC indicators manually. Quite often by the time you have worked all these out, the market has already moved and you will have missed your opportunity! Consequently there are two alternatives: you can either subscribe to a charting service or use the software system (supplied by the London School of Investment) and purchase either a BBC Micro, Amstrad PC/PCW, or IBM machine. Remember, when using the ROC indicator a level of 75 as an overbought signal can be high in a *bear* market but in a *bull* market an ROC of 80 may be more in line. It is very important to treat the charts for the ROC individually for each share, and study the back history of each chart to see how well it has worked in the past for that particular share.

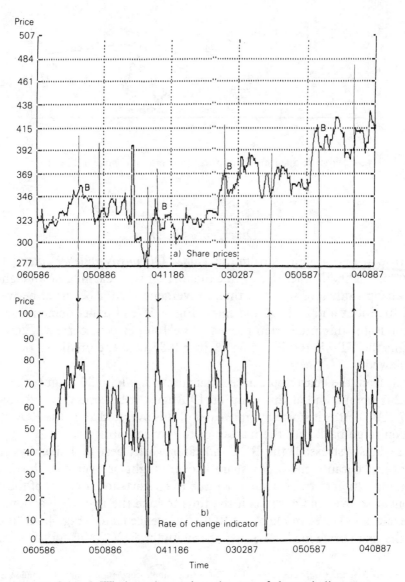

FIG. 4.53 Cable & Wireless: share prices plus rate of change indicator.

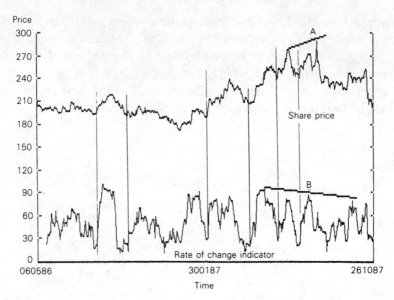

FIG. 4.54 Marks & Spencer: share prices plus rate of change indicator.

Divergence factor

The article in Fig. 4.55(a) is from the *Traded Options Newsletter** dated 13 July 1987. It highlights the fact that, while the market was reaching new heights, the rate of change indicator was not; thus a divergence factor occurred between the FT-SE 100 Index and its ROC indicator. Fig. 4.55(b) further demonstrates this.

On hindsight this prediction proved to be 100 per cent correct. Figure 4.56 highlights the FT-SE 100 Index on 13 July 1987 with the predicted down trend that followed.

In fact, from the chart you can see that from 13 July to 20 August the market fell by 201 points, and at this point on 19 August it became very oversold (at a level 27). As soon as it started to move out of this oversold area, the ROC gave an indication to go back into the market or to buy call options.

As previously stressed, the ROC indicator works best in a sideways-moving market. Just because the index share is overbought or oversold, this is not in itself an indication to react. *Only* when the ROC starts to move out of the critical overbought or oversold zones is it the time to take the necessary action.

If we take another example of the ROC divergence factor (Fig. 4.54), the chart shows the share price for M & S, together with the ROC indicator superimposed

Traded Options Newsletter is published weekly. For a free sample copy please contact: London School of Investment, 125 Gloucester Road, London SW7.

TABLE 4.4 Worksheet for ROC indicator.

Date	Close[1]	Up[2]	Down[3]	Up average[4]	Down average[5]	$\dfrac{\text{Up average}}{\text{Down average}}$ [6]	$x+1$ [7]	$\dfrac{100}{x}$ [8]	ROC[9]
1	372								
2	361		11						
3	354		7						
4	349		5						
5	345		4						
6	348	3							
7	358	10							
8	359	1							
9	365	6							
10	369	4							
11	360		9						
12	353		7						
13	348		5						
14	345		3						
Total		$\frac{24}{14}$	$\frac{51}{14}$	1.71	3.64	0.47	1.47	68	32
15	353	8							
16	358	3							
17	367	9							
18	368	1							
19	370	2							

1. Closing price on the day
2. Amount the price closed *up* from the previous day.
3. Amount the price closed *down* from the previous day.
4. Value of the average up closes. (Add all prices in column three and divide by 14.)
5. Value of the average down closes. (Add all the down closes and divide by 14.)
6. Result of dividing the up average by the down average
7. Result of adding one to number in column seven.
8. Result of dividing 100 by the number in column eight.
9. Value of ROC achieved by subtracting the number in column nine from one.

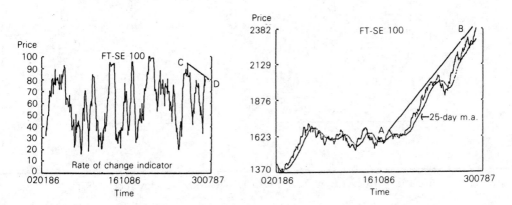

FIG. 4.55(a) Extract from *Traded Options Newsletter*, 13 July 1987.

MARKET POISED FOR A TECHNICAL RALLY!!

Although the US Congress is now making reassuring noises that it will reduce the budget deficit by $23bn, confidence will have to be fully restored before we see a long term rise in stock markets.

Mr Lawson suggested that a further reduction in interest rates could be forthcoming and the Government bonds rallied strongly earlier on in the week. Further gains in Gilts (recommended last week) are unlikely until the US deficit talks are satisfactorily concluded.

Rumours are now flooding in that President Reagan is going to make a statement on the 15 November which should give the markets an encouraging boost. I have also heard from

several market analysts predicting a technical rally is about to unfold.

Cadburys was a strong feature in the market on Tuesday rallying 30p on news that General Cinema have tried to increase their stake by another 10%.

Although the market still remains cautious, a significant increase in the buying of leading quality stocks by institutional investors began on Tuesday and looks set to continue.

Richard Hexton,

Technically, the market is looking very interesting. At present the market has found support at the 1600 level and if it can stay above this level for more than two days then we could see a strong technical rally, perhaps up to the 1750 level. IN ORDER FOR THE RALLY TO PERSIST, THE INDEX MUST CLOSE ABOVE 1620 BEFORE ITS NEXT DOWNTURN MOVEMENT, AND WHEN IT DOES TURN DOWN IT MUST NOT FALL BELOW THE LEVEL OF 1563.

I believe this is very possible and the chart shows the FTSE-100 Index together with its 4-day, 9-day and 18-day moving averages superimposed. If the 4 and 9-day moving averages can cross up through the 18-day moving average which in turn are all moving up, then a technical bull rally will follow. If it bounces away from its 18-day moving average then the bear market will continue. I opt for the former!

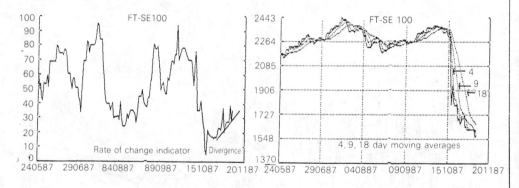

FIG. 4.55(b) Extract from *Traded Options Newsletter*, 12 November 1987.

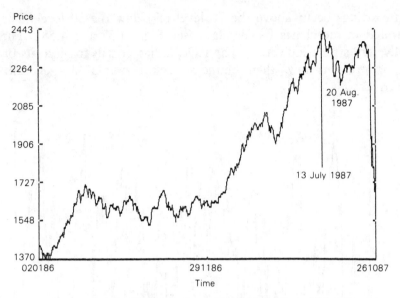

FIG. 4.56 FT-SE 100: index price highlighted on 13 July.

underneath. Again, we can see the M & S share price reading new highs at point A; but the ROC failing to do so is shown at point B, thus indicating that a reversal trend was about to set in. In fact, this happened immediately afterwards.

Summary

1. ROC is a momentum indicator and is basically telling you when a move is still accelerating and when it is slowing down.
2. It is measured between zero and 100.
3. The figure of 80 + might appear high in a *bear* market, but not necessarily so in a *bull* market. It is important, as with all other indicators, to interpret ROC in the context of the market and any other factors.
4. A divergence factor, rather than absolute level, is more important.
5. You should study the back history of the ROC to each particular share and see how well it has worked in the past. What is high for one share, say an ROC reading of 70 points, may be low for another share.
6. Only act when the ROC begins to move out of the critical overbought or oversold zone.
7. Often trends-chart problems, such as 'double bottom', 'double top', 'head and shoulders' and triangles, show up on the ROC indicator but not on the linear share price chart itself – thus highlighting that a reversal or continuation pattern is about to set in.

8. Failure swings occur above the 70 level or below the 30 level. These are illustrated in the charts for Barclays (see Figs. 4.57 and 4.58). There are usually very strong indicators. The ROC indicator fails to reach its previous high or previous low, then bounces back giving a buy or sell signal respectively.

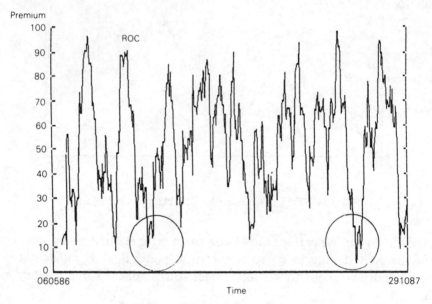

FIG. 4.57 Barclays: failure swings.

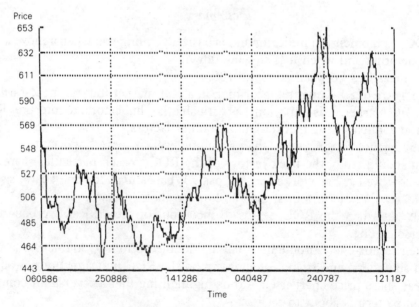

FIG. 4.58 Barclays: share price.

Overbought/oversold indicator

Earlier the use of a moving average was discussed. Now we will use an average in a different way, namely by measuring the distance between the moving average and the price of the share or commodity and deciding, if the distance is extreme, that the security is too high in a bull market or too low in a bear market.

When calculating the overbought/oversold index, the figure arrived at can be plotted either side of the zero line. In order to make the overbought/oversold effective, it is important to note a divergence between the price performance and the indicator. If the price leaps to a new high and the indicator does too, all well and good. If the price, after a pause, goes to another new high but the indicator does not, watch out! You now have a higher high in prices but a lower high on the indicator of a bearish divergence. This implies a loss of momentum.

A share price over 20 per cent apart from its 50-day moving average is judged to be at risk with an unsustainable momentum. There are all kinds of reasons why individual stocks do this, e.g. takeover bids. It is rarer for the whole market to move in this way. So, the more stocks in the top 500 that are either overbought or oversold, the more likely the stock market is to be heading for a short-term correction.

Figure 4.59 shows the overbought/oversold index for the FT-SE 100 Index, measured over a 14-day period, while Figure 4.60 shows the closing prices. Compare the two charts, highlighting the buy and sell signals.

The figures are usually calculated using a ten-day moving average of the difference between the number of shares rising and the number falling over a day's trading. (Shares which have been traded at overcharged prices are ignored.) Table 4.5 illustrates such a calculation.

For example, on the 11th day the number of shares rising is 30 and the number

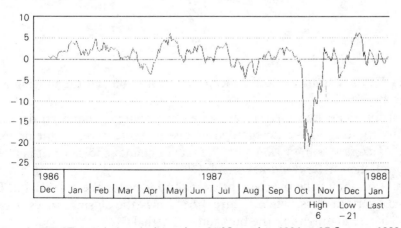

FIG. 4.59 FT-SE 100: index closing prices 21 November 1986 to 27 January 1988 I.

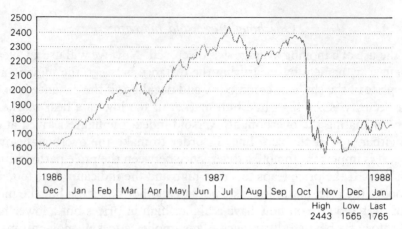

FIG. 4.60 FT-SE 100: index closing prices 21 November 1986 to 27 January 1988.

TABLE 4.5 Overbought/oversold calculation.

		Up	Down	Cumulative difference
Week 1	Mon	70	30	40
	Tues	80	20	100
	Wed	76	17	159
	Thurs	50	40	169
	Fri	40	60	149
Week 2		Up	Down	
	Mon	30	70	109
	Tues	20	60	69
	Wed	10	65	14
	Thurs	20	45	−11
	Fri	35	50	−26

10-day average = −26/10 = −2.6
(i.e. on average 2.6 shares fell each day).

falling is 70; the cumulative difference will rise to −66 and the moving average will then be −6.6.

Eventually, these moving average points are plotted around an oscillator at zero. Plus eight or above is regarded as overbought, minus eight or more as oversold. Taken in conjunction with the rate of change indicator, it is a reliable indicator of shorter-term market trends.

Figure 4.61 shows the overbought/oversold index for the FT-SE 100 Index, measured over ten days, while Figure 4.62 shows the closing prices. Compare the two charts, highlighting the buy and sell signals.

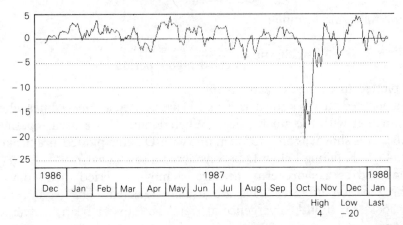

FIG. 4.61 FT-SE 100: overbought/oversold index calculation 21 November 1986 to 27 January 1988 II.

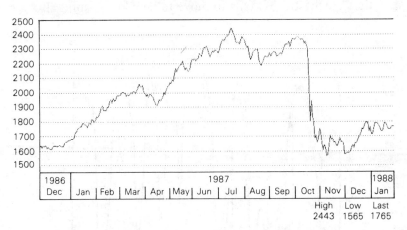

FIG. 4.62 FT-SE 100: index closing prices 21 November 1986 to 27 January 1988.

Stochastic process

Stochastic indicators tend to be most effective in evaluating price histories which show strong cyclical tendencies – in other words, shares which tend to oscillate between pronounced peaks and troughs within the overall trend. The stochastic indicator is usually very effective at pinpointing each peak or trough immediately before a price reversal occurs.

In its simplest form, the stochastic curve acts as a market momentum indicator, oscillating between a value of zero and 100. The principle behind the basic stochastic curve is that, as the price decreases, the lows tend to congregate closer to the extreme high. The stochastic curve is calculated on a moving basis, using the following formula:

$$stochastic = \frac{latest\ price - period\ low}{period\ high - period\ low}$$

and is plotted in a range of zero to 100.

The smoothed curves known as K and D are plotted as *broken* lines when used in conjunction with the stock price. (When K and D are used together as in Fig. 4.63, K is shown as an unbroken line with D being plotted as a broken line. In Fig. 4.63, K falling below D is considered a sell signal.)

When used as a short-term measure, a moving period of 14 days and a smoothing period of three days are usually selected. The technical analyst usually looks for bullish divergence at trend bottoms or bearish divergence at trend tops.

Bullish divergence occurs when the share price falls to a new low, whereas the single smoothed stochastic (K) fails to move to new low ground also (i.e. moves

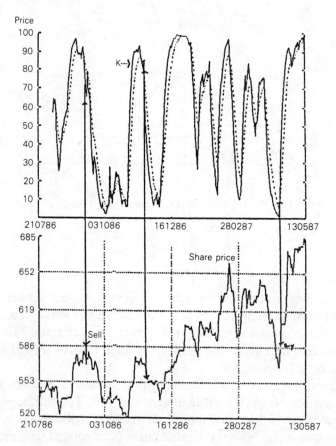

FIG. 4.63 Midland Bank: stochastic curve.

in an upward direction). The decision to buy is given on the day when the stochastic curve moves up through the K curve (broken line).

Bearish divergence occurs when the share price moves to a new high but the single smoothed stochastic (K) curve fails to rise in sympathy. The sell signal is given as the day the stochastic curve crosses down through the K curve.

Some technical analysts adopt a different approach utilising only the K and D curves. In this case K (unbroken line) rising above D (broken) line is considered a buy signal, and K moving below D is taken as a sell signal.

A 'double smoothing' effect comes into play when a three-day moving average of the raw stochastic is used, termed K, and a three-day moving average of K, called D. This 'double smoothing' eliminates a large portion of the minor niggles in the raw price data, offering the stochastic trader the ability to see more clearly the underlying price cycles in the market place.

Since the raw stochastic relates the current price to its relative position compared to the range of the past 14 trading days, the readings which vary from zero to 100 (as previously stated) make interpretation of K and D much easier. Buy signals are given when K rises above D, with sell signals generated by K moving below.

Examples

Let's now see stochastics working in practice. Figure 4.64 shows the share price for BT from 1 May 1986 to 13 May 1987. Underneath its share price you will find illustrated the

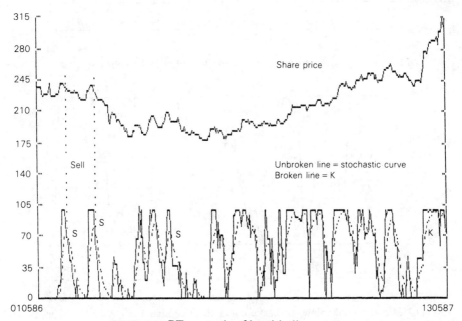

FIG. 4.64 BT: example of bearish divergence.

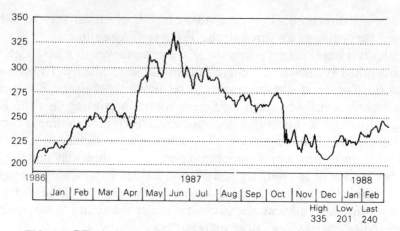

FIG. 4.65 BT: closing prices 16 December 1986 to 19 February 1988.

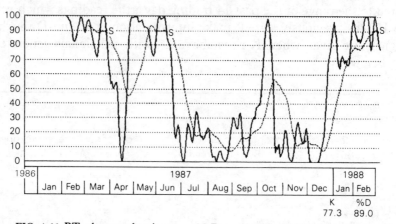

FIG. 4.66 BT: slow stochastic curve 16 December to 19 February 1988.

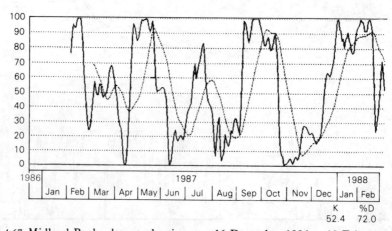

FIG. 4.67 Midland Bank: slow stochastic curve 16 December 1986 to 19 February 1988.

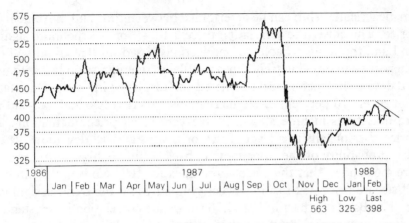

High Low Last
563   325 398

FIG. 4.68 Midland Bank: closing prices 16 December 1986 to 19 February 1988.

stochastic curve. As illustrated at points S, the sell indicator was given when the stochastic curve crossed down through the K curve (broken line).

See also Figs. 4.65 and 4.66. Fig. 4.65 shows British Telecom's closing share prices from 16 December 1986 to 19 February 1988, and Fig. 4.66 shows British Telecom's 'slow' stochastics chart during the same period.

Also illustrated is the 'slow' stochastics chart for Midland Bank. (See Figs. 4.67 and 4.68.) Many traders prefer this formula to the 'regular' stochastics chart. With the slow stochastics, the more sensitive percentage K line is dropped. The original formula for the regular percentage D line becomes the new slow percentage K line. The new slow percentage D line is a three-day moving average of the slow percentage line.

REGRESSION ANALYSIS: THE LONGER-TERM APPROACH

This system is used mainly by fund managers as a long-term approach. It is a good buy indicator, and, although it would be very laborious to calculate longhand, any computerised programme can cope with it very simply. Basically, the system fixes a trendline through the centre of the price formation, by taking the mean of all the prices plotted. The main use of the regression line is to identify when the price is moving away from the trend. The investor can draw parallel trend lines either side of the regression line, by drawing the typical peaks and troughs of the price curve. The stock is considered a good buy below the regression line, and an even better buy below the trend line.

The accuracy of the regression line is determined by the correlation index which can range from $+1$ to -1. A value of $+1$ indicates that as time progresses the share price will rise in perfect sympathy. A value of -1 indicates that the price will fall in perfect sympathy. A correlation value of zero means that no mathematical relationship can be determined between time and movement in the share price. The closer the correlation price is to $+1$ or -1 the more significant the trend and the more reliable any projections based on that trend will be.

An alternative to drawing trend lines parallel to the regression line is to use the standard deviation which is also calculated and displayed in pence. One standard deviation covers 76 per cent of all fluctuations, whereas two and two-and-a-half standard deviations include 90 and 95 per cent of all price fluctuations. If the share price rises or falls to a level of two or more standard deviations, then the statistical probability of the price moving back in line is high.

Figure 4.69 shows that the correlation index for ICI stands at 947, indicating that ICI's share price will rise in perfect sympathy and the trend is significantly reliable. The Barclays chart in Fig. 4.70 shows the correlation index standing at 650, indicating that the trend is not so reliable.

Not all aspects of technical analysis have been covered, since this would result in a separate book for this topic alone. However, some of the more important techniques used in technical analysis have been illustrated in relation to the traded options market and many worked examples in the retail market have been used so that you can see the charts worked in practice.

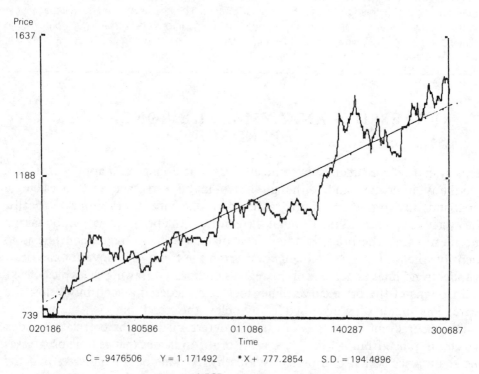

C = .9476506   Y = 1.171492   * X + 777.2854   S.D. = 194.4896

FIG. 4.69 ICI: regression analysis.

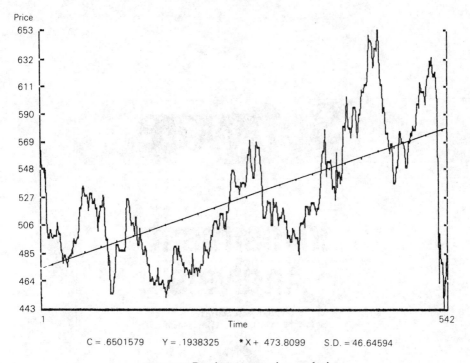

FIG. 4.70 Barclays: regression analysis.

Software

Investment
Analysts

**From Synery Software
and The London School of Investment**

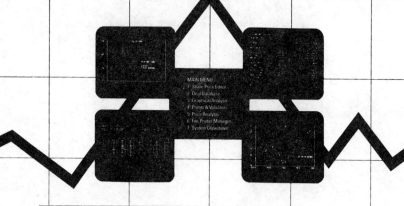

'a sophisticated combined portfolio and price graphics program . . . comprehensive and easy to follow' — **Investors Chronicle**

'[Synergy] has what appears to be the most comprehensive and cheapest product on the market'.
— **Daily Telegraph**

'An excellent package and good value for money. Highly recommended for the serious investor.'
— **London School of Investment'**.

'There's no reason why ShareMaster shouldn't grace the portfolio of every interested investor'
— **Complete Guide to the Amstrad PCW**

'The program represents value for money which does not seem to be equalled in its field' —
Acorn User

**The London School of Investment
125 Gloucester Road, London SW7 4TE**

FIVE

WRITING OPTIONS

INTRODUCTION

So far we have been concerned only with the *purchase* of traded options, and the investor subsequently selling them on in order (hopefully) to make a profit on his trade. Now we will look at the investor who decides to *sell* or *write* (whichever term you prefer) a traded option.

'Selling' or 'writing' traded options represents the other side of the coin in the options market. The writing of options plays a very important part. Whereas the buyer of a traded option *pays* a premium, a writer of a traded option *receives* a premium. However, in return for receiving this premium, the writer of an option incurs a *liability*. In the case of a call option, he is *obligated* to *supply* those shares to a holder of a call option who has exercised his right on the option contract. In the case of a put option, the investor who has written a put option incurs the *liability* to *purchase* the underlying stock at the exercise price chosen any time until expiry.

> Writing call options: Investor receives premium
> Writing put options: Investor incurs a liability

WRITING CALL OPTIONS

There are four basic rules for *call* option writing:

1. If an investor expects *little* movement in the price of the underlying security, he should write 'at-the-money' options, thus maximising the time value on the premium. *Time value works in favour of the option writer and against the option buyer.*

    So as time progresses, the time value attached to the premium sold (written) will become less and less, and the investor will be able to buy back the option at a cheaper price, and in return make a profit.

2. If the investor believes a price will *fall*, then he should write 'in-the-money'

options. (But any private investor should be well aware of his liability, which is open ended if he doesn't own the underlying security.) *Do not write 'in-the-money' options until you fully understand your liability.*

3. The option writer must always be prepared to accept being exercised by the buyer of the option. (Remember, the exercise price is the price for a share at which the buyer of a call or a put option may buy or sell the underlying security.) Exercise and assignment will be discussed in more detail later in this chapter.

4. If you are writing options without owning the underlying security, it is safer to write 'out-of-the-money' options, since there is less chance of being exercised by the purchaser of the options.

So why do investors write options? Let's look at writing call options. Investors tend to write call options when they anticipate that the price of the underlying security will remain steady or fall.

Covered call writing

'Covered' call writing implies that you already own the shares and are willing to give up the shares for a guaranteed maximum sale price.

Example: ICI

Let's suppose the investor holds 3,000 ICI shares at a price of 994p on 25 July. He feels in the present market that this is as high as the shares will go and he notices that the pound has been considerably strengthening against the dollar recently.

The investor decides to write three Oct contracts at an exercise price of 1,000, for which he receives 47p per contract. (Total received, $3,000 \times 47p = £1,410$.) So he now has the following alternatives:

1. To close his option by buying the options in the market back before expiry.
2. To let the options expire.

	Premium	Calls 26 July				Premium	Calls 1 August		
		Oct	Jan	Apr			Oct	Jan	Apr
ICI 994*	900	107	132	—	ICI 989*	900	105	132	—
	950	72	97	115		950	67	97	112
	1000	47	70	80		1000	40	67	77
	1050	22	47	57		1050	18	44	55

* Share price

Let us assume that on 1 August he decides to close his position. The share price has fallen from 994p to 989p – a fall of 5p. However, the premium he has received of 47p, less the buy back premium of 40p (assuming closing prices only), gives him a profit of 7p, before dealing

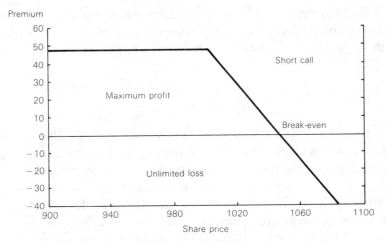

FIG. 5.1 ICI: writing a call option.

costs. So, at this point he would have been 2p per share better off by writing the option (7 − 5 = 2). (See Fig. 5.1.)

If he had let the option run to expiry, the 47p premium he received on writing the option would compensate for the loss sustained on the share down to a level of 947p (994p − 47p premium). Below this price, the loss on the shares would be greater than the profit on the options. But he would still be better off than by doing nothing! This is a good example of how traded options can be used for 'protecting' your portfolio. This type of strategy is known as 'covered' call writing, as opposed to 'naked' writing which is when you do not own the shares. In the latter case margins would have to be provided.

If, in fact, ICI shares started to rise instead of fall, and rose above the 1,000 price, the writer would be liable to be 'exercised' at an effective sale price of (1,000p + 47p) 1,047p. Only if the shares go above this price need you worry.

So, when writing options, 'time value' is to your advantage. As time evaporates, so the premium reduces, and the buy-back premium option is cheaper, thus leaving you with a net profit. *Remember when writing options, time works in your favour. When buying options, time works against you.*

Another consideration to be borne in mind is your expectations of the share price movement. Are you neutral, bearish or bullish? Your expectations will determine which exercise price you select. So, most writers tend to opt for 'out-of-the-money' options, and your view of the share price movement, will determine how deep an out-of-the-money exercise price you select.

So, if you are bullish about ICI or particularly keen to hold on to the shares, you might opt for the 1,050 October series. In this case your premium income is reduced to 22p per contract, and only in the case of the shares going above 1,050p will the option probably be exercised. The effective sale price would be

(1,050p + 22p) 1,072p. However, you will have less protection on the downside, as soon as the shares fall to 972 (994p current share price – 22p premium).

To sum up, covered call writing is a form of *protection* and is a conservative strategy.

Naked call writing

The other type of call option writing is 'naked' call writing. This is much more speculative, and it is certainly not recommended to the new investor, since the loss is unlimited and you need to watch the underlying security very closely. In addition, margins are required. So, if you are exercised in the market, when writing naked, you will be obliged to buy the shares in the market in order to deliver. Only write naked call options deep out-of-the money, and then only one or two contracts! Watch very closely. If you do not have the time or opportunity to write naked, we would advise against writing naked calls.

It is often the margin requirement that becomes too much, resulting in the writer being compelled to buy back the written option at a substantial loss. This is perhaps one of the most speculative methods of writing options and is the same as selling stocks 'short', i.e. selling stocks which you do not own.

WRITING PUT OPTIONS

Writing puts, like writing calls, creates a liability. In this case, you grant somebody else the right to sell a share to you at a fixed price. Unlike naked call writing, naked put writing is a completely different ball game, especially if you wish to acquire the shares.

Example: ICI again

Let's take a look at ICI again. You are seriously considering buying the shares at their current price of 994p but, if possible, would like to buy them slightly cheaper. So, if you write the October 1,000 puts, say at 50p, and the shares in fact fall instead of rise, you will probably be exercised and be obliged to buy the shares at 1,000. But, if you deduct the premium received (50p), your effective purchase price is 950p – still 44p cheaper than the original price.

However, if ICI should rise above 1,000, then you would neither be exercised, not be able to purchase the shares at the lower price, but you would have received 50p a share!

So, writing puts is very good, if you really wish to purchase the shares. To sum up, the call writer is a prospective seller of shares, while the put writer is a prospective buyer of shares.

If you wrote a call option on a share *XYZ* at an exercise price of 350p, for which you received a premium of 18p, your opinion might be that the stock was going to fall in price; and so in turn was the premium, thus enabling the writer to buy back the option at a cheaper price and so make a profit. Alternatively the call could expire worthless, i.e. if there was no intrinsic value attached to the option at expiry.

However, if you were wrong and the share started to increase in price, your loss would be *unlimited*. Eventually you would be exercised and you would have to buy in the stock to deliver.

Writing puts: In anticipation of an increase in share price
Writing calls: In anticipation of a decrease in share price

RULES FOR UNCOVERED WRITING

There are three basic rules worth remembering which are as follows:

1. Be very careful of writing 'in-the-money' option series. If in doubt – stay out. It is suggested that the private investor should *not* use this strategy.
2. If the written option appears to have gone wrong, close your position immediately.
3. Remember – 'writing naked' incurs an *unlimited* liability.

LOCH

All option transactions are registered by a computer called LOCH (London Options Clearing House) and exercise is a random process. However, never write options unless you are in a position to deliver.

LOCH is a wholly owned subsidiary company of The Stock Exchange and is responsible for the registration and settlement of all traded option transactions. There is no direct link between the buyer and seller of a traded option contract once their transaction has been registered by LOCH. For every current holder of an option contract, however, it is axiomatic that there must be a writer who has a similar open position, and so the total of the outstanding contracts held by buyers must equal the number of contracts for which writers are responsible. LOCH acts as a registrar for these open contracts on behalf of The Stock Exchange and, when a holder exercises a contract, LOCH appoints by a process of random selection a writer of a contract in the same series to deliver or receive the shares in accordance with the terms of the contract.

If the holder of options wishes to buy or sell the underlying security, exercise notices are issued to LOCH by the client's broker. LOCH will, on the following day, issue an assignment notice to another broker requesting that his client, the option writer, fulfils the terms of the option contract. Bargains are then settled on the appropriate settlement day, i.e. the account day for stock options, the next business day for gilt and index options and the third business day for currency options. 'Exercise and assignment' is dealt with in more detail later in this chapter.

TERMS USED IN OPTION WRITING

Opening sale

The writer of a traded option contract is said to make an 'opening sale', e.g. a sale to open three contracts of ICI 1,050 October series at *x* premium.

Closing purchase

If a writer of a traded option contract re-purchases in the market in order to close his position he makes a 'closing purchase', e.g. buying to close three contracts of ICI 1,050 October series at *x* premium.

Margins

If you are writing naked, you will be required to lodge a 'margin' with your broker. A margin is required from all option writers. It is based on the percentage value of the underlying stock, plus or minus the amount by which the exercise price is in or out-of-the-money. Basically, you take 20 per cent of the value of the underlying security and either add on the amount by which the option is 'in-the-money' or subtract the amount by which it is out-of-the-money.

In the example of ICI (assuming writing naked), the investor writes three ICI 1,000 option contracts when the stock stands at 994p

20 per cent of 994	= 198
Deduct out-of-the-money element	= 6
Margin required	= 192p
Margin per contract 192 × 1,000	= 1,920
For three contracts	= 5,760

You may use cash, gilt-edged stock or underlying securities. These margins are calculated daily as the share price movement changes as follows:

Equities	= 20 per cent margin
Index	= 12.5 per cent margin
Gilts	= 5 per cent margin
Currencies	= 8 per cent margin

Margins have to be put up by 10.00 a.m. on the morning following the transaction day.

Out-of-the-money margin requirement

For example, for British Telecom 200 call options:

Market price = 185$_p$
Margin   = 20 per cent × 185 = 37$_p$ − 15$_p$ (200 − 185)
       = 22 × 1,000 = 220p per contract

In-the-money margin requirement

For example, for British Telecom 180 call options:

Market price = 185$_p$
Margin   = 20 per cent × 185 = 37$_p$ + 5$_p$ (185 − 180)
       = 42 × 1,000 = 420p per contract

Exercise and assignment

When a holder exercises his option, an assignment notice is issued to a writer of an option contract in the same series of options, instructing him to deliver the underlying security to the exercisor. The actual operation of delivering the shares is handled by the brokers of the two clients through the normal Stock Exchange settlement system.

Once an assignment notice has been received by the writer of an option contract, he may not close his position in the option market but must provide the shares called, either by delivering his existing holding or by purchasing the required shares in the market.

The day following the submission of the exercise notice, the broker will issue to the buyer a contract note stating the number of shares he has purchased at the exercise price stated. The assignee's (seller's) broker will issue a contract note stating that he has sold the same. Settlement will be on the account day of the dealing period then ruling.

Whilst a low margin requirement allows the possibility of high profits, the daily adjustment of margin can make this exercise very expensive in terms of tying up capital. The investor must always remember to calculate the loss on interest he would have required from the capital sum on deposit against the potential profit from premiums received. Don't tie up high capital sums for low effective premium returns. The margin requirements could become enormous if the market moves strongly against the writer.

A further example of ICI

As illustrated below, a rise in the market price of an underlying security against a call written naked can have an effect on the margin requirement and so reduce returns on the investment:

Exercise Price	(A)	= 1,000p (out-of-the-money)
Market price	(B)	= 994p[*]
Margin 20 per cent of	(B)	= 198p
Less difference between market price and exercise price		− 6p
Actual margin		= 192p × number of contracts × 1,000
Premium received		= 47p
Return		= 24 per cent

[*]Share price

Share rises		
Exercise price	(A)	= 1,000p
Market price	(B)	= 1,050p[*]
Margin 20 per cent of	(B)	= 210p
Plus difference between market price and exercise price (in-the-money)		+ 50p
Actual margin		= 260p × number of contracts × 1,000
Premium received		= 47p
Return		= 18 per cent

[*]Share price

PRACTICAL HINTS FOR WRITING NAKED

It is advisable to do the following before attempting to write naked:

1. Study the nearer dated option cycles, e.g. towards the end of November look at the options that expire in December (Beecham, Boots, BTR, Bass, Blue Circle etc.).
2. Study the share price history over the last few months, and try to establish a trading pattern. Ask yourself whether the share is in a downward or upward trend, is overbought or oversold and what the mood of the market is generally.
3. When you have reached a decision about the future possible price movement of the underlying security, decide whether to write calls, puts or combinations and straddles (explained in the next chapter).
4. Try and select the out-of-the-money nearer dated series, with premiums that have a high time value. Remember, time value works in favour of the seller.
5. Work out your margin requirement before dealing.

6. Once you have dealt, watch your premiums closely.
7. Always be aware of the dealing costs involved. Often the premiums received for writing the options may be too low to warrant the potential profit after dealing costs have been taken into consideration.

Example: Jaguar

Date: 4 December
Share price: 520p
Write Dec 500 puts for 4p × 5 contracts
Margin: (104 − 20) = 84p × 5,000 = 4,200
Profit on expiry at share price of 520p = 200p (4p × 5 × 1,000)
Dealing costs: Minimum dealing cost of 20p to open and 20p to close a transaction + £1.50 per contract + VAT

Example: Thorn EMI

Date: 1 December
Share price: 473p
Write Dec 460 puts for 5p × 5 contracts
Margin: (95 − 13) = 82p × 5,000 = 4,100
Profit on expiry at share price of 475p = 250p (5p × 5 × 1,000)
Dealing costs: Minimum costs and fees (as above)

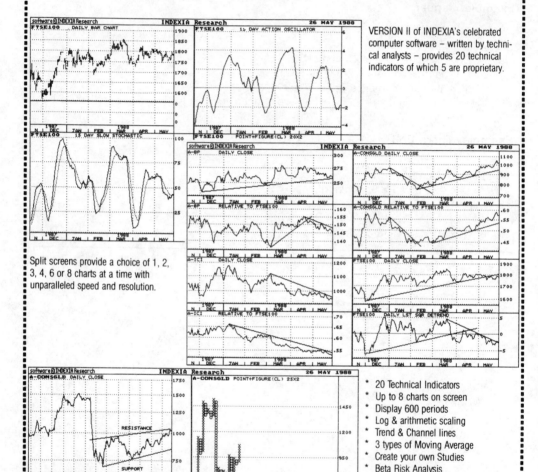

SIX

TRADED OPTION STRATEGIES

SPREAD STRATEGIES IN A KNOWN MARKET

Introduction

Spreads are used for reducing risk. A number are available to the investor, and shown below with worked examples are some of the more common trading strategies that can be used to take advantage of existing market conditions. It is only proposed, however, to introduce you to the more popular ones, since complicated spreads can often incur extra expenses and result in unwanted assignments. As an investor in the options market you should always ask yourself what you are trying to achieve and what your expectations are of the movement in the underlying share price. If a large movement is expected, then writing options is *not* the answer; whereas if a small movement is anticipated, writing options could be the answer. Alternatively, the investor might decide to deal the option because it is dearer or cheaper in relation to another series in the same class. In this case, some kind of spread might be used.

What is a spread?

The primary objective of a spread transaction is to *reduce risk*. Typically, a spread transaction consists of buying one option contract (going long) and selling another option contract (going short) on the same underlying security. These two positions together make up a spread.

As you will remember from previous chapters, a purchase of an option requires a payment from the investor, while the sale of an option results in a credit to the investor (less margin requirement, where applicable). So, if you pay out more than you receive, your spread will have a debit and you will have 'bought the spread'. Alternatively, if you receive more than you pay, you will have a credit and you will have 'sold the spread'.

Profit or loss

Profit or loss on a spread results from the price difference between the two options increasing or decreasing, as the price of the underlying stock changes and time passes.

Examples: *XYZ*

Let's take a basic mathematical example of option *XYZ* and see how the spread works:

(a)	Option series	Price	Stock price
	XYZ Dec 50	6p	45p
	XYZ Dec 80	3p	45p

Investors buy a spread

Buys *XYZ* Dec 50 at 6p debit
Sells *XYZ* Dec 80 at 3p credit
Net debit = 3p

Now let's see what has happened to the spread a few weeks later after a rise in price in the underlying security:

(b)	Option series	Price
	XYZ Dec 50	12p
	XYZ Dec 80	5p

If you look at the figures in (a) the difference in price between the two options is 3p, whereas in (b) it is 7p. So let's have a look at your result, if you were now to sell back the option you previously bought and buy back the option you previously sold:

(c)	*XYZ* Dec 50	*XYX* Dec 80
	Bought at 6p	Sold at 3p
	Sold at 12p	Bought at 5p
	Profit = 6p	Loss = 2p
		Net profit = 4p

N.B. These examples exclude dealing costs and differences between bid-offer premiums.

However, if you had simply purchased Dec 50 calls at 6p and sold for 12p, you would have made a gain of 6p instead of 4p using the spread.

Why spreads?

The main reason for using spreads is to reduce risk; but in return for reducing risk, the investor will also limit his profit.

If instead of rising *XYZ* had, in fact, started to fall, the maximum loss at expiry on the spread would have been 3p (6p – 3p (a)). But in the case of buying the *XYZ* Dec 50 calls for 6p, the potential loss would have been 6p. Thus by spreading you would reduce your risk by 100 per cent.

Now, let's look at some spreading strategies.

Vertical bull spreads

The features of a vertical bull spread are:

(a) the same expiry date
(b) different striking prices.

These are used when the investor believes that the underlying market/stock will move higher but wishes to limit initial outlay as much as possible. The extent of one's bullishness will determine the exercise price chosen – ideal for a technical rally in an oversold security.

Example: Shell Transport

An investor anticipates a rise in Shell Transport from its current price of 768p to a level not exceeding 800p.

Spread: Buy 750/800 spread for a net debit of 21p

(In-the-money) buy 750 July calls at 28p Debit
(Out-of-the-money) sell 800 July calls at 7p Credit
Net debit = 21p

Figure 6.1 shows the result of opening the spread for a net cost of 21p (difference between purchasing the 750 calls at 28p and the amount received from selling the 800 calls at 7p).

Break-even: Lower strike price + net cost 771p   = 750p + 21p
Maximum profit at expiry if share price reaches 800p = 29p
Maximum loss at expiry if share price is below 750p = 21p

Profits or losses can be calculated from Fig. 6.1 between share prices of 750–800p.

We have now established that a profit occurs if the share price exceeds 771p at expiry (750 – lower striking price + net cost of spread – 21p).

If Shell rises to 800p, then the July 750s, which the investor bought for 28p, now have an *intrinsic* value of 50p, plus possibly some time value, whilst the July 800s would only be worth whatever time value is left in the market.

Let's analyse the profit or loss situation on the spread if both positions were closed out just before expiry:

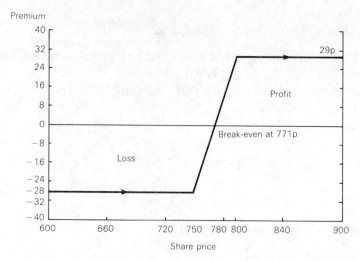

FIG. 6.1 Shell: vertical bull spread.

Option series	Option series
July 750s	July 800s
Bought at − 28p	Sold at + 7p
Sold at + 51p (50p intrinsic value, 1p time value)	Bought at − 1p
Profit = + 23p	Profit = + 6p
Total profit = 29p (23p + 6p)	

When selecting vertical bull spreads, try to use nearer dated options, i.e. if the date of trading is June, look at those options with July expiry dates, or if the date of trading is August, use those options in the September series.

Many investors will not enter into a vertical bull spread unless they can buy it for a debit of 40 per cent or less of the difference between the exercise prices. You should also ideally search out stocks with tight dealing spreads, since you may have to complete four transactions to close the position.

In the previous example of Shell, the exercise prices of the two options (750 and 800) are 50 points apart, so a vertical bull spread would only be considered if it would be opened for a debit of 20p (40 per cent of 50).

Criteria
The following factors should be taken into consideration:

1. **Risk factor.** Many investors will not enter into a vertical bull spread unless they can buy it for 40 per cent or less of the difference between exercise prices.

2. Risk/reward ratio. The risk/reward ratio should not be more than 2/1 against you.
3. Volatility. The percentage move in underlying stock is also a vital consideration, unless there is enough volatility present in the stock to make a profit. (In the above example of Shell a 39 per cent movement in the underlying stock is required.)

Thus by purchasing a call with a lower exercise price and selling a call with a higher exercise price, the object is to reduce the cost of the purchase; this in turn reduces the appreciation in the underlying security to make a profit.

Diagonal bull spreads

The diagonal bull spread strategy is ideal when you are bearish to the reaction of the market/equity in the short term, but bullish in the medium to long term. It again involves the simultaneous sale and purchase of two call options, in this case with different dates and exercise prices.

In effect, it is a matter of selling out-of-the-money near-dated calls and buying in-the-money further-dated calls. Don't forget that the idea behind spreads is to reduce the risk of your capital outlayed, whilst at the same time producing high percentage profits.

When using nearer-dated out-of-the-money options, you should therefore be looking for those option premiums with most time value attached to them – since, when writing options, time erosion works in your favour. But when buying the longer-dated in-the-money options, the premiums shouldn't be overvalued.

The features of a diagonal bull spread are:

(a) different expiry date
(b) different striking prices.

It is used when the investor is bullish in the medium term, but slightly bearish in the short term. The investor's price expectations would range from neutral to mildly bearish.

Example: Commercial Union

Stock price: 236p
Date: December
Write (sell): January 240 calls at 11p
Purchase: April 220 calls at 29p
Cost: Spread opened for a net debit of 18p (29p – 11p)

At January expiry shares were still trading at 236p so the 240 series expired worthless and the

11p per contract was pocketed. The April 220 calls were now held for a debit of 18p.

The market then picked up and the April 220 calls were finally sold for 110p bid at a net profit of 92p (+ 511 per cent!). An ideal situation for a diagonal spread.

Summary

If the short-expiry written option wastes to zero at expiry, then the investor will have purchased the longer-dated call for an effective net reduction in the longer-dated call.

The out-of-the-money option written short-term is unlikely to give a great deal of protection, if the share price falls dramatically to start with. It is therefore advisable to effect diagonal spreads when you expect price movements to be neutral to mildly bearish to start with.

Vertical bearish spreads

The investor will establish 'bear' spreads when he is 'bearish' of the market/ equity. The purchased option will have a strike price higher than the one sold. Vertical bear spreads are the mirror image of vertical bull spreads. Their features are:

(a) same expiry date
(b) different striking prices.

A bear spread involves the *sale* of an 'in-the-money' call option, e.g. against a purchase of an 'out-of-the-money' call option. It can be used when the investor feels that the price of a stock will go down but wishes to reduce his risk on the outright short position (*writing in-the-money*). The advantage of the vertical bear spread, is that the investor has covered his potential unlimited loss on the uncovered call should the stock rise rather than fall.

Example

An investor anticipates a fall in the UK Market, from its current level of 1,630 (FT-SE Index) to a level not exceeding 1,600.

Spread

Buy 1,650 July puts at 35p
Sell 1,600 July puts at 12p
Net debit = 23p

Figure 6.2 shows the result of opening the spread for a net cost of 23p (the difference between purchasing 1,650 July puts at 35p and the amount received from selling the 1,600 July puts at 12p).

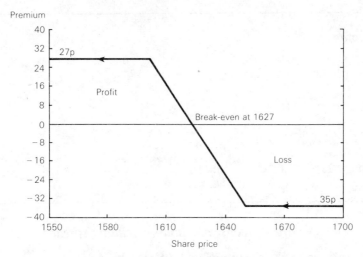

FIG. 6.2 FT-SE 100 Index: bearish vertical spread.

Break-even: Higher strike price − net cost 1,650p − 23p = 1,627p
Maximum profit: At expiry if share falls to 1,600p = 27p
Maximum loss: At expiry if share rises to 1,650p = 23p

Once again we have established that a profit occurs if the FT-SE Index falls below 1,627.

If the FT-SE falls to 1,600, then the July 1,650 puts which we've bought for 35p, now have an intrinsic value of 50p (a gain of 15p); whilst the July 1,600, sold for 12p, would expire worthless at expiry showing a gain of 12p. The total gain for the spread would be 27p (15p + 12p).

Again, when selecting put spreads, it is better to use nearer-dated options, since the time value to expiry will erode more rapidly than with longer-dated options. The next stage is to study the worksheet involved in assessing the vertical *put* spread strategy.

Criteria
Let us now analyse the factors that have to be taken into consideration:

1. Risk factor: 23/50 = 46 per cent
2. Risk/reward: 23/27 = 85 per cent
3. Stock movement to make a profit: 3/1630 = 0.18 per cent

The risk factor was around the 40 per cent mark (50 per cent or less is justifiable). The risk/reward ratio is 23/27, i.e. you risk 23p to make 27p. This is a little high, but only a very small movement of the index is needed to break-even (0.18 per cent).

In reality, let us see what actually happened.

Example contd

On 16 July the FT-SE Index had fallen to 1,596 (so there was still time value left in the premiums of the options).

To close spread

Buy July 1,600 puts at − 16p
Sell July 1,650 puts at + 60p
Net credit = 44p
Profit: 44p − 23p = 21p (210 per contract)
Percentage return on investment: 21/23 = 91 per cent

Neutral spreads and time (calendar) spreads

These spreads involve the simultaneous sale of a short-dated call and purchase of a longer-dated one. They require neutral price expectations for the underlying stock. The principal features are the wasting away of the time value of the short-dated option with the longer-dated one returning its premium.

If the share price remains static, the effective cost of the longer-dated option is reduced, or the spread will have widened, giving the investor a useful profit.

The features of these spreads are:

(a) different expiry date;
(b) same striking prices.

They are used when the investor expects the stock will remain in a flat or neutral position. The general theory underlying a time spread is that as time passes the spread will widen, i.e. the spread between the two most distant months will be less than the spread between the two nearest months. A general rule for neutral time spreads is: sell short, buy long, at-the-money exercise price.

Time spreads
Again, you can be bearish or bullish, but these spreads are particularly suited to stock which is in a neutral position.

Sell short: Maximum time value
Buy long: Minimum time value

Examples of bullish time spreads

Sell short, buy long, out-of-the-money.

Stock price: 35p
Exercise price: 40p (April and July series)

Buy the July 40s for 5p (buy long)
Sell the April 40s for 3p (sell short)
Net debit = 2p
Stock moves up to 40p
July 40s = 4p (time value left till July)
April 40s worthless = (expired)
Profit = + 2p

How bullish you are depends on how far out-of-the-money you write the option.
Let's take a look at the following example and use bullish time spreads for Commercial Union:

Option		Calls			Puts		
	Premium	July	Oct	Jan	July	Oct	Jan
Commercial Union 310*							
1 July	280	36	44	—	2	6	—
	300	17	31	38	5	13	15
	330	4	17	26	20	25	28
Option	Premium	July	Oct	Jan	July	Oct	Jan
Commercial Union 318*							
17 July	280	38	43	—	1	3	—
	300	18	29	39	2	9	12
	330	1.5	15	24	14	22	24

* Share price

1 July: buy the October 330 for 17p and sell the July 330 for 4p.
17 July: close the October 330 at 15p (− 2p) and close the July 330 at 1.5p (+ 2.5p).

This requires more movement in bullish time spread than writing a combination does. Therefore, remember, when 'writing' time works in your favour, so, unless there is a more substantial rise in the stock, or more volatility, the combination written will be more profitable than the bullish time spread.

Example of bearish time spreads: sell short, buy long, in-the-money

These are not advisable, since the theory of time spreads is based on the time value of a short option diminishing more rapidly than that of a long option.

Stock price: 45p
Sell short April in-the-money 40s for 8p
Buy long July in-the-money 40s for 9p
                                     − 1p
Stock moves down to 40p Profit/loss
April series expires worthless 8p
July series 4p − 5p
Net profit = 3p

With bearish time spreads watch the possibility of being exercised. Since bearish time spreads usually involve the use of in-the-money options, the time values involved tend to be relatively small.

Let's study the following example.

The FT-SE Index on 21 March 1986 stood at 1,688 and the overbought/oversold (ROC) indicator stood at 91p demonstrating that the index was very overbought and due to fall.

Sell the May 1,625 calls for 118p
Buy the June 1,625 calls for 130p
Net debit = 12p

Therefore, if the market is weak in May, you can benefit from the sale of the 1,625 calls, reaping the premium and going for a rally at a later date.

Sell the nearer-dated and buy the longer-dated: the short nearer-dated option diminishes more rapidly than the longer option. The short option *must* have a large time value (e.g. May 1,625 with index at 1,688:

intrinsic value = 63p
time value = 55p

So, at the end of May the FT-SE Index stood at 1,612 and the 1,625 May series would have expired worthless, thus keeping all the 118p premium. The time 1,625 calls would not have any intrinsic value left, but with a time value of, say, 30p the net profit would be 18p per contract.

Remember that to be successful in calendar spreads requires neutral price expectations for the underlying stock. Investors are well advised to restrict their activity in time spreads to out-of-the-money series, since early assignment of in-the-money or at-the-money series, is a distinct possibility.

TABLE 6.1 Margin requirements for spread strategies.

Purchased option	Margin required
Same or later expiry date with same or lower striking price than option written	None
Same or later expiry date with higher striking price than option written	Difference between striking prices
Earlier expiry date than option written	Full margin on option written

SPREAD STRATEGIES IN AN UNKNOWN MARKET

Introduction

There are also strategies available to investors who are not sure in which way the underlying security will move. The only thing the investor is convinced of is that the share price will fluctuate. 'Straddles' or 'combinations' are strategies that will accommodate the investor's indecision.

Buying a straddle

This involves the simultaneous purchase of a call option and put option on the same share with the same exercise price. The investor should be convinced that a sharp movement of the share price will occur in either direction.

The investor will only make a profit if the movement, in either direction, generates a premium high enough to exceed the premium paid for the spread.

Example: Beecham

The share price of Beecham is 440p on 3 July. (Again, for simplicity, we shall ignore dealing costs and assume the bid and offer prices are the same.) There is a bid rumour of a takeover for Beecham, but at the same time the trend in the UK market is very bearish. So, the investor expects a sharp movement in Beecham's share price but is uncertain of its direction.

The investor, therefore, decides to purchase a straddle:

Share price: 440p
Buys Beecham 460 Sept calls at 22p
Buys Beecham 460 Sept Puts at 33p

Total cost (debit)   = 55p

To realise a profit at expiry, the price of Beecham must be below 405p (460 − 55p), making the puts worth more than 55p, or above 515p (460 + 55p), making the calls worth more than 55p.

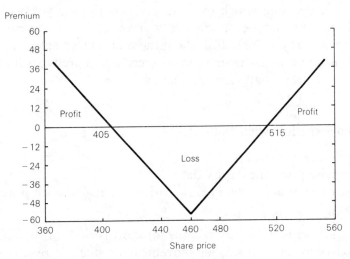

FIG. 6.3 Beecham: straddle.

Assume the stock at expiry is 535p. The puts will expire worthless; but the calls will be worth 75p. Since the cost of the straddle was 55p, the profit is 20p per contract (75p−55p) × 1,000. Break-even for the straddle at expiry is as follows:

Call 460 exercise price + cost of straddle (55p) = 515p
Put 460 exercise price − cost of straddle (55p) = 405p

Referring to Fig. 6.3, unless the price of the stock at expiry is *below* or *above* the break-even points, a straddle held until expiry will not realise a profit. If it is *between* the break-even points, a loss will be incurred. The maximum loss will occur if the share price closes near or at the exercise price of 460p.

On 16 July Beecham's share price was 418p − a fall from 440p. Let's now see what happened to the option premiums:

	Profit/loss
Sept 460 calls at 12p	− 10p
Sept 460 puts at 50p	+ 17p
Net profit =	7p

Which straddle

Having decided to buy a straddle, the next question to answer is whether to buy short term or long term? A short-term straddle costs less, and therefore requires a smaller movement in the stock price to make a profit. A long-term straddle has the advantage of more time to make a profit but requires a larger increase in the stock price movement to do so. Generally, the longer-term straddle justifies the extra cost.

Again, when deciding which exercise price to choose, you will usually be confronted with an exercise price slightly above or below the current market price of the stock. If you are bullish about the price movement of the stock, then choose the *call*, that is, in-the-money; whereas if you are bearish of the stock, choose the *put* option, that is, in-the-money.

Summary

Straddles have the following features:

1. Minimum time value.
2. Same exercise price and expiry date.
3. Purchase of a put and a call in anticipation of a major stock price movement either way.

A point to consider is the expiry month? (a) short period? or (b) long period? A short period costs less, so smaller movement of stock is required. A longer period costs more, but has the advantage of allowing more time in which to make a profit. If the stock price doesn't move sharply, the loss will be less with a shorter expiry date. While if the stock price does move sharply, more profit will be made in percentage terms providing it moves before the expiry date. But remember! A longer-term option is usually more justifiable.

Buying a combination

This involves the simultaneous purchase of an out-of-the-money call option and an out-of-the-money put option on the same share with *different* exercise prices and/or expiry dates. Combination writing is more geared to low price movement and/or volatility than purchasing time spreads.

Profit will only occur if the movement, in either direction, generates a premium high enough to exceed the premium paid for the spread.

Why a combination?

Why buy a combination rather than a straddle? Looking at Beecham, the investor can compare risk factors and chances of profit and loss situations, plus any gearing effect the combination can have against the straddle used.

Example: Beecham

See Fig. 6.4.

Share price: 440p

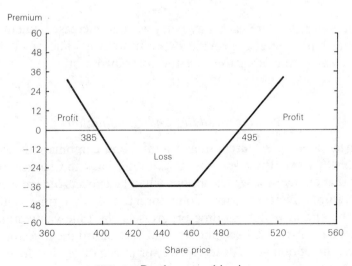

FIG. 6.4 Beecham: combination.

Buy Beecham 460 Sept calls at 22p (out-of-the-money)
Buy Beecham 460 Sept calls at 13p (out-of-the-money)

Total cost (debit) =   35p

so the combination, at a total cost of 35p, is 20p cheaper than the straddle. However, it involves a greater chance of losing all your investment.

At expiry, total loss occurs between 420p and 460p, whereas with a straddle total loss occurs only if the share price remains at 460p until expiry.

Break-even is 460p + 35p = 495p
Break-even is 420p − 35p = 385p

(Break-even for the straddle was 405p − 515p.)

Features

Combinations have the following features:

1. Minimum time value.
2. Different exercise prices and/or expiry dates.
3. Purchase of a put and a call in anticipation of a major stock price movement – either way.
4. Lower cash outlay than a straddle, but usually higher risk.

For example:

Stock price: 250
Purchase Feb 250 calls at   18p
Purchase April 200 puts at   6p

Total outlay   =   24p (debit)

Basically, these spreads are each way bets, with an increased amount of capital requirement; but they also provide extra insurance. The stock must move *strongly* one way or the other to cover the combined cost.

Writing straddles and combinations

We have been looking at purchasing straddles and combinations. Now we will look at *selling* (*writing*) these spreads. If you refer back to Chapter Five you will remember that an investor writes options when he expects *little* movement in the price of the underlying security. Don't forget, too, that time value works in favour of the option writer: as time progresses, the time value attached to the premium sold (written) will become less and less and so the investor will be able to buy back the option at a cheaper price, or alternatively let the option expire worthless.

So, now let's look at writing spreads.

Writing a straddle
The main features of writing a straddle are:

(a) same expiry date;
(b) same striking price;
(c) maximum time value; and
(d) little movement in share price, usually written out-of-the-money.

Example 1:   Trafalgar House

The share price of Trafalgar House is 293p on 4 July. (Again, for simplicity, ignore dealing costs and assume the bid and offer prices are the same.) There has been very little movement in the Trafalgar House share price and so the investor feels that the share price will not alter substantially. (See Fig. 6.5.)

However, this particular ploy is more suited to the *holder* of the stock, since the likelihood of the share price remaining in a very restricted band is remote and unwanted assignment could occur. Low volatility is essential to realising a profit on a written straddle.

> Date: 4 July
> Share price: 293p
> Write 280 July calls at   18p
> Write 280 July puts at   3p
> Total credit: 21p

(N.B. A bearish spread, since the July 280 calls are written in-the-money and the puts are written out-of-the-money.)

> Maximum profit at expiry: 280p
> Profitable between: 301p and 259p
> Break-even call: 301p (280p + 21p)
> Break-even put: 259p (280p − 21p)

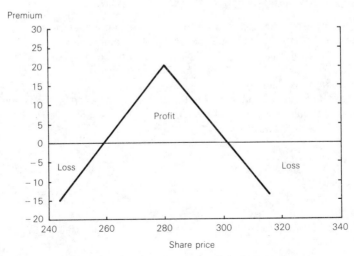

FIG. 6.5 Trafalgar House, written straddle.

If the share price at expiry closes at 280p, both options will expire worthless, and all the premium received (21p) will accrue to the writer. At a level of 301p, the call options written will have an intrinsic value of 21p. Hence, if an assignment is deemed undesirable, these will have to be re-purchased at this intrinsic value. Similarly, if the share price fell, the writer would have downside protection to 259p (280p − 21p), with 1p for 1p losses below this level.

Let's see what actually happened to the profit/loss situation on the straddle. Ten (trading) days later (14 July) the share price had moved to 281p (a fall of 12p) and the situation looked like this:

	Profit/loss
280 July calls at 8p	+ 10p profit
280 July puts at 7p	− 4p loss
Net profit =	+ 6p

Fourteen (trading) days later (18 July) the share price had moved to 275p (a fall of 18p) and the situation was as follows:

	Profit/loss
280 July calls at 3p	+ 15p profit
280 July puts at 9p	− 6p loss
Net profit =	+ 9p

Example 2: Hanson Trust

Date: 4 July
Share price: 185p
Write 180 Sept calls at 15p (in-the-money)
Write 180 Sept puts at 7p (out-of-the-money)
Total credit: 22p
Maximum profit at expiry: 180p
Profitable between: 158p and 202p
Break-even call: 202p (180p + 22p)
Break-even put: 158p (180p − 22p)

In this example, Hanson Trust options are dealt in the September series whereas Trafalgar House options were dealt in the July series. Both examples were written in July. The nearer-dated options with maximum time value tend to favour the option writer. If you refer back to Chapter Two, you will remember that time value erodes more quickly as an option moves towards its expiry date.

Again, let's see what actually happened to the profit/loss situation on the straddle written for Hanson Trust. Ten (trading) days later (14 July) the share price had moved to 181p (a fall of 4p) and the situation looked like this:

	Profit/loss
180 Sept calls at 10p	+ 5p profit
180 Sept puts at 8p	− 1p loss
Net profit =	+ 4p

Fourteen (trading) days later (18 July) the share price had again fallen, this time by 12p to 173p:

	Profit/loss
180 Sept calls at 7p	+ 8p profit
180 Sept puts at 11p	− 4p loss
Net profit =	+ 4p

Writing a combination

The main features of writing a combination are:

a) different strking price and/or expiry date;
b) writing a call and a put;
c) maximum time value; and
d) little movement in the share price, and usually written out-of-the-money.

Example 1

See Fig. 6.6.

Share price: 144p
Sell Aug 150 calls at 13p (out-of-the-money)
Sell June 135 puts at   6p

Credit   19p

Maximum profit at expiry: between 135p and 150p
Break-even for call: 169p (150p + 19p)
Break-even for put: 116p (135p − 19p)
Profitable: Between 116p and 169p

(N.B. If you are bearish of the stock, write in-the-money calls and out-of-the-money puts.)

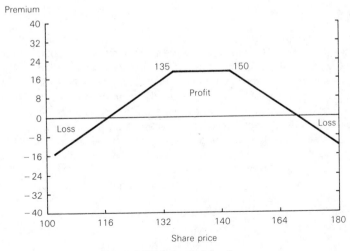

FIG. 6.6 Writen combination.

Example 2: ICI

Share price: 971p

Sell July 1,000 calls at 14p (out-of-the-money)
Sell July 950 puts at   13p (out-of-the-money)
Total credit   =   27p

Maximum profit at expiry is achieved if the share price closes between 1,000 and 950, when both options will expire worthless. Break-even is achieved when the share price rises to 1,027p (1,000p + 27p) for the calls, and if the share price falls to 923p (950 − 27p) for the puts. Again, it is important for the investor to keep a careful eye on the options at a level above 1,000p and below 950p.

It is very important to remember that dealing costs and spreads of options can have a dramatic effect on your profits, especially if the option premiums written are small.

Lifting a leg and running naked

'Lifting a leg' is a term used when dealing in spread strategies. It is best explained by the use of a diagonal spread which was bought for a debit in Allied Lyons.

Example: Allied Lyons

Buy Oct 330 calls at 37p (in-the-money)

Sell July 360 calls at 6p (out-of-the-money)

Total debit =   31p

If the investor decides to close either side of this spread and leave the other running, this is known as 'lifting a leg'. In this particular case, the investor closed the option purchased and was left as a naked writer of the July 360 calls. Hence, the term 'lifting a leg and running naked'.

Within two weeks of the purchase of the diagonal spread the share price of Allied Lyons had risen by 31p to 363p. However, technical analysis of the option showed that Allied Lyons' share price had reached the top of its trend channel and was becoming overbought at a rate of change indicator of 86 − an indication that the share price would drop.

In this instance, the alternatives facing the investor were either to hold on to the diagonal spread until expiry, with the 360 calls expiring worthless at the end of July, thus pocketing the 6p premium and staying with the October 330s for a net debit of 31p, or to lift a leg.

So, the investor now closes the October 330 calls for a bid price of 50p, showing a profit of 13p for contract before dealing costs, lets the July 360s run naked and put up the required margin − since the written call is no longer covered by the longer-dated October 330 calls.

Within three days the share price of Allied Lyons actually dropped to 338p, and the 360 calls were closed at 7p for an overall gain on the spread of 12p per contract.

Sometimes the investor may even decide to re-establish a leg which has been lifted. If he believes the underlying stock is on the verge of another price rise, then by re-purchasing the same option which had previously been sold, the investor can once again establish the spread.

Spreads require careful selection and calculation and should be watched at all times. They are a useful tool for reducing risk, but deserve the necessary time and attention to make them profitable.

MARGIN REQUIREMENTS

The margins shown in Table 6.1 (p.122) are the minimum margins required for spread strategies, but often money brokerage firms request their customers to put up more than the minimum margin.

PROFIT OR LOSS ON A SPREAD

Again, the profit or loss on a spread results from the *price difference* between the two options increasing or decreasing as the price of the underlying stock changes and time passes. (See also p. 114.)

Example XYZ

Let's take the example of the XYZ stock and see how the spread works:

(a)

Option series	Price	Stock price
XYX Dec 90	15p	100p
XYX Dec 110	4p	100p

Investor sells a spread

  Sells the Dec 90 for 15p
  Buys the Dec 110 for 4p
  Net credit = 11p

(Margin requirement in this case would be the difference between two exercise prices of the option series, less the credit received from the spread itself.)

Let's see what happened to the spread a few weeks later after a fall in the price of the underlying security.

(b)

Option series	Price	Share
XYX Dec 90	1p	91p
XYX Dec 110	Cabinet*	91p

*See Glossary.

(c)

XYZ Dec 90	XYZ Dec 110
Sold at 15p	Bought at 4p
Bought at 1p	Sold at 0
Profit = 14p	Loss = 4p
	Net profit = 10p

If you had simply sold short (written naked on XYZ Dec 90 at 15p) and the options had expired worthless, you would have had a profit of 15p instead of only 10p. However, the purpose of spreads is to *reduce risk*. If the stock had risen instead of fallen, your loss would have been unlimited in a naked written position, whereas with the spread it is limited to (20p − 11p) = 9p per contract.

Example: Dixons

An investor anticipates a fall in Dixons from its current price of 329p.

Spread

Sell 300/330 spread for a net credit of 28p
Sell 300 Dec calls at 34p credit
Buy 330 Dec calls at 6p debit
Net credit = 28p

Again, by the use of the worksheets the investor can assess the profit/loss situation in the vertical bear spread chosen.

Let us now analyse the profit and loss situation on the spread, when Dixons had fallen to 319p eight days later:

300 Dec calls at 20p
330 Dec calls at 1p

So, the 300 Dec calls could have been bought back for 20p (profit of 14p) and the 330 Dec calls sold for 1p (loss of 5p), with a total profit of 9p per contract × 1,000 (ignoring dealing costs of bid-offer premiums).

Alternatively, you could have let the spread continue and, if Dixons had continued to fall in price, the maximum profit of 28p per contract might have been achieved.

TRANSACTION COSTS

Transaction costs should always be monitored against the overall potential profit situation. Since spreads involve at least twice the number of contracts as a simple long or short position and are also closed out before expiry, transaction costs can run high and erode any profit realised.

TRADING SUMMARY

There are innumerable option trading strategies each with its own combination of risk and return. An investor should choose that which gives the maximum return should his expectations be fulfilled, conditional on an acceptable level of risk. Transaction costs and margin requirements must always be considered when planning option trades.

So, options provide a sophisticated mechanism for tailoring return distributions very closely to the investor's price or volatility forecasts.

TIPS FOR THE INVESTOR

Theory, practice and information are the three vital factors to bear in mind, when dealing in the traded options market.

1. Theory: Understanding the theory is very important – not only the basic principles of what a call option is, or whether a put option can make money in a falling market, but, more importantly, understanding the various strategies that exist to help you reduce your risks, such as combinations, straddles, butterflies.

    It is also important to realise that premiums become overvalued and that by using the Black–Scholes formula (see Chapter Seven), you can work out whether you are paying a fair price for the option premium.

    Quite often the stock moves but the premium doesn't – simply because the latter has been overvalued at the time of purchase. It is vital to understand that when writing naked your liability is unlimited, whereas when purchasing options your liability is limited to the premium paid.

2. Practice: when you first enter into the market, tread carefully: you are going to make mistakes and, hopefully, learn from them as well. The London School of Investment has devised an ingenious course that not only gives you all the theory in a series of lecture notes, but also, perhaps more importantly, allows you actually to deal in the real traded options market through their simulated programme. You can simply ring them up and treat them like a broker. They will give you £10,000 monopoly money to play with over a twelve–week period, so that you can experience the dealing costs involved, understand how premiums become overvalued, and see how bid and offer premiums on options play an important part in the market.

3. Information: the right information is very important. Read your *Financial*

Times daily and the *Financial Weekly*. Use either The Stock Exchange's Market Eye for obtaining up-to-the-minute option prices, or alternatively the Prestel CitiService system (see Appendix 1).

You should know your stocks in detail, including:

(a) the fundamentals – use research that includes details of forecast profits and dividends, together with the overall buy/sell/hold recommendations;

(b) the trading sentiment – many stocks have predictable trading patterns: bank shares, for example, tend to have a rally in the period approaching results; charts give a surprisingly clear picture of this;

(c) technical ranges – research shows the technical support and resistance levels on option stocks: these are chart-based; very often, unless there is a good reason, stocks tend to move up and down within the trading range;

(d) volatility ranges – these should also be researched and when used in conjunction with trading ranges can be useful: at the top end of a trading range, and with rising volatility and bearish fundamentals, you should, for example, buy puts; at the top of a trading range, with high and falling volatility, you should write calls.

When you first start just open a few contracts at a time; then, once you have built up your confidence and have some profits behind you, you can start to be a little more aggressive and adventurous!

SEVEN

WHEN IT PAYS TO KNOW THE THEORY

CALCULATING THE THEORETICAL VALUE
OF AN OPTION

The theoretical value of an option presents its fair value. It is calculated by the use of advanced mathematics. Various parameters are used in these calculations, but market sentiment cannot be allowed for in a mathematical formula. An option is overvalued when the market price is more than its theoretical value; similarly an option is undervalued when the market price is less than its theoretical value.

Every penny in the share price of an option represents £10 per contract (of 1,000 shares). A typical deal might consist of four or five contracts. Thus, if an option is overvalued even by 2p, the investor would have paid £20 per contract more than he should have done or about £80 to £100 more on a typical deal. On the other hand, an option which is undervalued by 2p could save the investor £20 or more. It is, therefore, not only useful but potentially very profitable for the investor to know the theoretical price of an option.

For example, if an option is heavily overvalued the investor may decide:

(a) not to buy the options at that price;
(b) to sell that option, thus taking advantage of the situation; or
(c) to use some combination strategy, involving the sale of the overvalued option and the purchase of an undervalued option.

If an option is heavily undervalued, the investor may decide:

(a) not to sell the option at that price; or
(b) to buy that option.

There is usually no shortage of opportunities in the volatile traded options market. Market-makers do not always change all the option prices whenever there is a change in the stock price.

It is very important for the investor to know before dealing whether an option is over- or undervalued. If you look at the table for Glaxo (Fig. 7.1), you can see

Glaxo Holdings		1742.00 price			date 24091987	
	Dec	Mar	Jun	Dec	Mar	Jun
Call delta				Put Delta		
1700	0.65	0.67	0.69	0.35	0.33	0.31
1750	0.57	0.61	0.64	0.43	0.39	0.36
1800	0.48	0.56	0.60	0.52	0.44	0.40
Call prices				Put prices		
1700	131.3	192.3	243.7	60.7	84.5	101.5
1750	104.0	165.1	216.9	82.5	105.3	121.4
1800	81.0	140.8	192.4	108.4	128.8	143.6

Dividends (p)		Interest Rates			Call	Margin per Contract £ Strike	Put
XD Date	Net	Gross	Dec	9.73%	3904	1700	3064
23111987	7.00	9.59	Mar	9.66%	3404	1750	3564
11051988	5.00	6.85	Jun	9.63%	2904	1800	4064
28.06% Volatility		Margin 20.00%				Min. Margin 522.60	

FIG. 7.1 Theoretical premiums for three option cycles.
Source: Micro Minerva Consultants.

clearly demonstrated the theoretical premiums for three option series, both for calls and puts. These premiums can be compared with the actual premiums quoted to determine whether the premiums represent a fair price.

VOLATILITY

There are three basic types of volatility: *future* (anticipated) volatility is unknown but can be forecast; *historical* volatility is the actual volatility measured over a specific period of time; and *implied* volatility is derived mathematically from actual premiums by working backwards through a pricing model. Historical and implied volatility can be used to estimate future volatility, which is used as an input to option pricing models.

DELTA

Delta is a key concept in options theory. It is a measure of the option's price movement in response to a one-point change in the underlying index. The delta for a call option is a *positive* number between zero and one, while the delta for a put option is a *negative* number between zero and minus one. A call delta of 0.5 indicates that for a one point increase in the index the call should increase by half a point.

For both puts and calls, delta tends to increase as the option moves in-the-money and decreases as the option moves out-of-the-money. At-the-money call options normally have a delta near 0.5 and in-the-money options generally have a delta greater than 0.5.

THE BLACK–SCHOLES FORMULA

In May 1973 in an article called 'The Pricing of Options and Corporate Liabilities' published in the *Journal of Political Economy*, Fischer Black and Myron Scholes combined the elements of share price, volatility, time and interest rates in a complex mathematical model which attempts to determine the theoretical true value of a call option. It is widely used by professional option dealers and stockbrokers to search for situations in which the price appears to be different from the value. The formula is as follows:

$$P_0 = P_s N(d_1) - \frac{E}{e^{rt}} N(d_2)$$

where

$$d_1 = \frac{\ln(P_s/E) + (r + \tfrac{1}{2}o^2)t}{o\sqrt{t}}$$

$$d_2 = \frac{\ln(P_s/E) + (r - \tfrac{1}{2}o^2)t}{o\sqrt{t}}$$

and where:

P_0 = the value of the option
P_s = the current share price
E = the exercise price of the option
e = 2.71828
t = the time (in years) remaining before expiration
r = the current rate of interest
o = the volatility of the stock
$\ln(P_s/E)$ = the natural logarithm of (P_s/E)
$N(d)$ = the normal distribution function of d

Only the more mathematically inclined will understand how the formula is derived and it is, in fact, probably too difficult to remember. However, as it is kept on stockbrokers' computers and they (occasionally) publish research based on the formula, it is worth illustrating a simple example.

Example

Suppose the share price:

P_s = £36
E = £40
t = 0.25 (i.e. three months)
r = 0.05 (i.e. 5 per cent per annum)
o = 0.50

The values of d_1 and d_2 are thus:

$$d_1 = \frac{\ln(\frac{36}{40}) + (0.05 + \frac{1}{2}(0.50^2))0.025}{0.50\sqrt{0.25}} = -0.25$$

$$d_2 = \frac{\ln(\frac{36}{40}) + (0.05 - \frac{1}{2}(0.50^2))0.25}{0.50\sqrt{0.25}} = -0.50$$

We can then look up in a normal distribution table (which can be found in most statistics textbooks) to find $N(d_1)$ and $N(d_2)$.

$N(d_1) = N(-0.25) = 0.4013$

$N(d_2) = N(-0.50) = 0.3085$

So, from the original Black–Scholes formula we can find the value:

$P(36 \times 0.4013) - (40 \times 0.3085) = £2.26$

Of course, you would not normally be required to do all this, but a hand calculator could easily be programmed to do it.

This formula can be used in two ways: first, as above, where the value is found from the inputs; secondly, you can put in the price of the option as quoted in the market and, keeping all the other variables the same, find a measure for the volatility of the stock. If the formula says that the volatility of the stock is higher than you think, it means that the price of the option in the market is higher than you think it should be, and thus you should sell it or at least not buy it!

So, by the use of the Black–Scholes formula the price of an option can be assessed and its theoretical value established. Market-makers work on theoretical values taken from computer programs, and often manipulate option premiums to the point where they either become over or undervalued. Then eventually the market price of an option does come into line with its theoretical value. The investor, when dealing, should always try to buy *undervalued* options and sell *overvalued* options.

Table 7.1 lists a printout of the theoretical values for Blue Circle Mar series. It shows that at a share price of 703p, the theoretical value of the 700 calls was 24p

TABLE 7.1 Theoretical values
of Blue Circle Mar series.

Call	Theory	Bid	Ask
Mar 500	203	203	208
550	153	153	158
600	103	103	108
700	24	33	38
750	7	17	22

(middle price), so the dealing quotes should have been, say, 26p to 22p. However, in this case they were overvalued by 11.5p, and thus the stock would have had to move a great deal more than an undervalued option, in order for the investor to show a profit.

PROFITING FROM OPTION PRICE ANOMALIES

If it is possible to find overpriced and underpriced options on the same share, why not try to profit from this anomaly and avoid the share itself entirely? Hopefully, this is what we try to do with an option spread.

A 'price spread' is the purchase of one option (which we think is cheap) and the sale of another (which we think is dear), on the same share with the same expiry date but with a different exercise price. A 'time spread' involves the purchase and sale of options on the same share with the same exercise price but with different times to expiration.

In both these cases we would have to be able to calculate the value of the option very accurately. An investor could try to use the Black–Scholes model. One spread for which a mathematical model isn't needed, however, is the 'butterfly spread'. This involves selling two calls and buying two, one either side (in-the-money) of those sold. If the calls sold are priced higher than the calls bought then a guaranteed profit is made!

The following example will demonstrate this.

Example: Racal

Option	Premium	April calls
Racal	180	38
	200	22
	220	2

Here two April 200 calls could be sold for 2p (ignoring bid/offer spread and dealing costs), one April 180 could be bought for 38p, and one April 220 could be bought for 2p. So, what is the total cost?

$$38p + 2p - (2 \times 22p) = -4p$$

i.e. 4p profit.

But what happens if the calls are exercised? Imagine that the Racal price at the end of April is less than 180p. What happens? Absolutely nothing! No one will exercise their calls because the exercise price is above the market price. Thus total profit = 4p.

If the Racal price ends up above 220p what happens? Our investor with the 'butterfly' spread will find that he has 2,000 shares 'called away' at 220p. But he can buy 1,000 at 180p with a 20p profit and 1,000 at 220p with a 20p loss. The result of exercising all the options is that the investor comes out neutral, so again the total net profit = 4p.

What happens at prices between 180p and 220p? (Remember, the butterfly spread investor does not exercise his 220 calls.)

Here we have made a profit from dealing in the options and not bothering about the underlying share price! This really is a strategy for the professionals, though if you can do it – well done!

EIGHT

A BROKER'S VIEW

INTRODUCTION

This chapter has been written by Bob Foster-Moore who has turned an interest in traded options into a full-time career. He has set up a traded options department within Allied Provincial specialising in options for the private investor. He brings to this book his theoretical and practical knowledge together with his experience as an investor. It is hoped that this will prove both instructive and interesting in that firstly it demonstrates how an individual can develop an interest into a career and secondly it provides a checklist of criteria for selecting a stockbroker.

PERSONAL BACKGROUND AND EXPERIENCE

The launch of British Telecom shares was the event that led me to a fascination with the stockmarket. It seemed incredible that it was possible practically to double one's money in a matter of a few weeks! Two realisations, however, soon struck home:

1. That massive percentage increases do not occur frequently on shares.
2. That the capital required to obtain a respectable absolute profit on a more normal 10 per cent appreciation on a share price would be extremely high, e.g. the requirement of a £500 absolute profit level on ICI, assuming a 10 per cent appreciation from £10,000 to £11,000, would require a capital investment of £5,000.

These two factors resulted in my search for an investment medium that provided significant profit potential with limited risk and that required a relatively small capital outlay. This led me directly to traded options as satisfying the criteria above.

My first transaction as a private investor was in August 1985 involving a total of £300. In the two and a half years to date from this first deal in options I have been able to achieve a 700 per cent profit from my initial capital of £1,000. In retrospect, I went through three distinct phases of experience.

Phase One: Relying on other people's recommendations

The first few transactions proved profitable and were undertaken on the recommendations from a newspaper. I did no form of studying or research work myself to ensure that I personally felt totally happy about entering these positions. As it transpired these transactions were profitable, leading directly to Phase Two.

Phase Two: Assuming a profit is easy

I made the error of assuming that to make a profit from traded options was easy. I therefore opened positions of my own choosing, without studying the share or relying on a 'professional's' recommendation. The result was that I lost my previous profits, together with a small part of my starting capital.

Phase Three: Study

I now knew that significant profits or losses were obtainable via traded options; I had experienced both. Phase Three was the determination to make profits not losses. I realised that the only way to achieve this was by learning all that I could about options. This has made me realise the limitation of my knowledge; each book/article/discussion introduces more areas for learning, rather than increasing the areas learned.

My approach was sound but, with the benefit of hindsight, could have been significantly improved (see 'Lessons learned' below). Specifically, I undertook a study campaign as follows:

1. I took on a subscription to a traded options newsletter (*Richard Hexton's Options Monitor*) – a cost which has proved to be my most valuable investment.
2. I took out a subscription to two traded options chart services.
3. I read widely – initially, articles and books on traded options and, subsequently, books on technical analysis.
4. I studied an options course at the London School of Investment. I should have taken this course far earlier because it combines all the details of trading in options in one package – the only alternative is newspaper clippings, etc., resulting in disorganised information, and thus of little practical use.
5. I bought a computer and software. This finally enabled me to undertake the calculations and graphs necessary for the technical analysis of shares –

impossible without a computer. It provided me with the information to make my own investment decisions and to satisfy myself on other people's recommendations.

By this time I had developed some knowledge in a very specialist area of stockbroking but was still working for a firm of soap powder manufacturers (Procter and Gamble). I duly approached the stockbroker who was executing my transactions with the proposition of my setting up a department specialising only in traded options. I duly joined Allied Provincial in July 1987.

Lessons learned

Before discussing 'Frequent investor errors' as seen by a stockbroker, I should like to outline some of the lessons that I have learned. It may well prevent you from falling into similar predicaments. (Each of the following sections is discussed more fully under 'Frequent investor errors' below.)

Insufficient knowledge
It quickly became apparent that the investment decisions that I was making were based on very little knowledge of technical analysis or understanding of traded options. The result was a larger number of complete losses which seriously affected my total profit position. Additionally, I started to feel that my investments were controlling me, rather than vice versa.

Being sure of an investment
I occasionally felt that I had made the wrong investment decision almost as soon as I had entered the position. Patently, this is an unsettling feeling and left me concerned that I had made a mistake. In short, I was not convinced that it was right to open the position in the first place.

Stop losses
Had I employed a rigid stop loss system from the beginning, the total profit picture would have been dramatically improved. I found it almost impossible to close a position that was showing a loss, preferring to hope it would improve. The result was almost invariably a total loss.

Letting profits run
There were many situations in which I closed positions because I had made a profit and was scared that I would lose it. I had thus taken an emotional, rather than factual, decision to close and frequently saw positions that I had closed go on to make huge profits.

Trading levels

On one occasion I invested more capital in the market than I had available. There were two implications attached to this:

1. I was worried about the consequences of the positions going wrong.
2. I 'panicked' out of profitable positions too early, realising only small gains. My trading tactics were influenced almost entirely by fear of making a loss, rather than a clinical approach to making profits.

The examples cited are of mistakes that I have personally made. My experience as a stockbroker tends to show that many investors are making similar errors. I therefore propose to discuss each area at greater length with additional points not covered above.

FREQUENT INVESTOR ERRORS

Insufficient knowledge

Many investors incorrectly assume that it is easy to make a profit from traded options. They invest substantial sums without fully understanding either the investment positions themselves, or their implications. There are two fundamental requirements for trading options profitably:

1. Determining the direction of the share price.
2. Having the knowledge to identify which option or option strategy to utilise.

The most important step, therefore, is to acquire knowledge. This should be done prior to *any* form of investment in the market place.

Technical/fundamental analysis

You may choose to base your forecast of the underlying security price action on technical or fundamental analysis, or a combination of both. Whichever route you choose, it is essential that you institute a system for yourself that provides you with an above average chance of predicting share price movements correctly. Patently, a vast knowledge of options will be of little use unless you can correctly estimate the direction of the share price.

Fundamental analysis is based upon information regarding a company's historic and present performance. Technical analysis, however, is based purely, upon historic share price movements. Technical analysis has the advantage of showing you on paper day-by-day exactly how buyers and sellers are interacting, thereby giving pictorial buying and selling signals. Assuming that you agree that technical analysis should play at least a major role in predicting price movements, your starting point should be a comprehensive study of this area. There are excellent courses and numerous books on this fascinating subject. In retrospect, I would have done well to study this area fully prior to investing in options; it would have eliminated many of my mistakes.

You will also quickly discover that to use technical analysis effectively requires a host of mathematical calculations. A computer and specialist software ('Sharemaster' is excellent value for money) is vital. The sooner you determine to purchase a computer, the better. The alternative is to attempt a mass of mathematical calculations and plot graphs manually. This will leave little time for you to study your graphs and make investment decisions.

Knowledge of the options market
Having studied and gained a good understanding of likely share price movement, the next step would then be a study of options themselves. There are courses and books that specialise in this subject. The more you read, the greater your understanding of the total area.

General reading
In order to keep abreast of intended or current investments, it is essential to read a quality newspaper daily and to supplement this detail with other material (e.g. *Financial Weekly* or *Investors' Chronicle*).

Being sure of your investment

I frequently sense that investors are uncertain and unsure of their proposed investment positions. Prior to an investment decision you should do your own research. Obviously, listen to other people's comments and recommendations and then make up your own mind. It is fatal to invest in a position in which you yourself are uncertain – it means that you are not *convinced* by the reason to open the position. If you are uncertain, do not invest.

Stop losses

I have seen many investors allow their investments to expire worthless. They have allowed hope of a recovery in the position to overcome the fact that it was going wrong. Invariably the situation gets to the point where it is no longer worth closing out. You should always write down your own stop loss limits and stick to them rigidly. Many traders position stop losses at a support or resistance level on their charts. I would advocate that you place a percentage stop loss (20–25 per cent) on the bid price at the time of opening the position.

Assuming that the trade moves profitably, you should then move your stop loss so that it trails the rising bid price. Under no circumstances should you allow a profitable position to move into a loss, i.e. once the bid price is equal to the ask price originally paid you should close on any reaction to that price.

If you have a rigid stop loss system your losses will be limited. On many occasions, however, I have seen investors fall into the trap of taking profits too quickly. The net result is the incurring of small losses, and also small profits resulting in an overall small loss or gain. If a position becomes profitable, do not close it until there is a specific reason to do so. The technique of a trailing stop loss allows your profits to run whilst giving you the peace of mind that your stop loss is moving higher with each move in the share price. Peace of mind is important; judicious setting and use of stop losses takes away the daily questioning of 'What should I do now?' and makes your investment mechanical.

Trading levels

Money management is crucial to success. I have seen some investors invest more than they can afford to lose and the results have been disastrous. Isolate a trading fund that, if totally lost, would not drastically affect your life-style. Never invest more than you can afford to lose. Once this fund is established divide it into equal portions. Some traders use a division of three, others five and yet others ten. The important point is to work to a strictly regulated financial plan. The value of the divisions selected should increase or decrease according to accrued profits or losses. At no time should you have more positions open than the prearranged number. If you are fully invested and wish to open a new position, you are compelled by this financial plan to close an existing position. This introduces the excellent practice of re-assessing current positions in the light of new opportunities.

Averaging a loss

There are those who believe that, having purchased an option at say 50p, the same option at 30p represents a bargain. They duly average down their losses only to find that the option value declines still further. Their error has been the assumption that the share price *must* improve. Invariably it does just the opposite. Once you have taken a position, therefore, never invest more capital into that same position. The original investment decision might prove incorrect.

Don't despair

Any investment can become emotionally draining – traded options particularly so because of their volatility and gearing. The use of technical analysis and stop losses will reduce your 'emotional wear and tear'. They will help to ensure that the probabilities of profit will remain firmly on your side. I can only say that I have experienced both the highs of significant profits and the awful lows of continuing losses.

SUMMARY OF THE IDEAL LEARNING PROCESS

The following is a summary of points so far raised:

1. Understand technical analysis: take an investment course, read widely and buy a computer and software.
2. Understand traded options: take a course, subscribe to newsletters (see 'Further reading', p.190) and subscribe to chart services.
3. Read widely: the *Financial Times, Daily Telegraph, Investors' Chronicle, Financial Weekly,* Technical Analysis Course (see p.190).

SUMMARY OF DO'S AND DON'TS

The following is a short checklist learned by personal experience:

1. Knowledge levels: ensure a full understanding of technical and fundamental analysis, buy a computer and ensure a full understanding of traded options.
2. Be certain of your intended investment: make sure you are investing for good reasons.
3. Set firm stop losses: write them down and stick to them rigidly.
4. Let your profits run: only close when there is a reason to do so.
5. Have a total financial plan for your investment: ensure you are operating to a strict financial plan.
6. Never average down a loss: if the initial decision is wrong, cut your losses. Never invest more in a position that is going wrong.

HOW TO SELECT A STOCKBROKER

Investment/deposit level

Many firms have strict requirements regarding minimum investment levels, transactions per year, or the placing of a minimum cash balance as deposit. You may be required, for example, to deposit £5,000 to undertake at least 50 transactions per year, or to undertake transactions on at least five contracts. You may immediately determine that these stipulations do not suit your requirements.

Qualifications

The first step is to ensure that the firms you are contacting are members of The Stock Exchange. If so, they are regulated by The Stock Exchange. The impact on you is that all your transactions and any dealings are carried out under strict controls.

Accessibility

It is essential that you are able to contact your stockbroker as required: it is useless having an excellent stockbroker unless you are able to discuss your investments with him. Make sure, therefore, that he is easily contactable and that he 'phones you back if unavailable.

Knowledge and expertise

You should satisfy yourself that he has a high level of knowledge and expertise in the field of traded options.

Ask him (a) how he makes investment decisions; (b) how long he has had experience of the options market; and (c) about the more complex option strategies (e.g. ratio spreads/butterflies, etc.).

Satisfy yourself that he does have the necessary knowledge and experience to help you.

Contact

This may well prove to be the area that separates one broker from another. There are many brokers who will not contact you on their own initiative. They will only discuss positions if you contact them or ask them to contact you. The broker with whom you should deal is the one who takes the initiative in contacting you. If he is the type of broker who routinely contacts his clients, you should then investigate the following areas.

Current open positions

Establish whether he will keep you in contact with your open positions. Will he contact you to say that you should consider closing a position, and, if so, be prepared to discuss his reasons?

Control of stop losses and profit-run parameters

Ask whether he operates any system of stop loss and profit parameters. When you open a position you should investigate if he will accept a stop and profit loss figure. You should also understand how the system would work in practice.

The ideal situation would be one whereby you and the broker agree a stop loss and a profit level on opening a position with the stop loss trailing the premium upwards as the option advances. This gives you the security of knowing that your losses will be limited, whilst your profits will be allowed to run.

Recommendations

Establish whether the firm publishes a traded options newsletter and, if so, at what cost. Ask him if he is prepared to contact you directly with recommendations. Ask him on what criteria these recommendations will be based.

Efficiency

Does he appear to be efficient? Investigate how quickly transactions are carried out, when contract notes are dispatched, etc.

Charges

This should be the least area of concern. It is far more important to receive specialist advice and service at a slightly higher cost than it is to receive a low standard of service at a low cost.

Obviously, you should ascertain the firms' charges and use them as part of the decision-making process of which broker to select.

As a guide, most brokers have a minimum commission charge of £20 or two and a half per cent of the consideration, whichever is the larger. Some brokers offer special terms for closing or spread transactions.

Attitude

At the end of a discussion covering the above points you will be able to ascertain what attitude the broker has towards his clients; whether he is going to try to help you or whether he is only interested in taking your instructions.

It would be advisable to have a checklist of questions to ask your potential, prior to contacting him. Once your have talked with all the brokers you plan to contact, you will then be able to compare checklists and reach a decision on which appears to offer the best service.

A suggested checklist appears below.

STOCKBROKER QUESTIONS CHECKLIST

1. Required investment: Is there a minimum investment/deposit level?
2. Qualifications: Is the firm a member of The Stock Exchange? Is the individual fully qualified?
3. Accessibility: Is he easily contactable? Will he return your call if unavailable?
4. Knowledge and experience: How does he make investment decisions (technical/fundamental analysis)? How long has he had experience of the options market? How detailed is his knowledge of the more complex option strategies (e.g. ratio spreads/butterflies)?
5. Contact: (a) Current open positions: Will he keep you informed? Stop loss and profit levels: Is there a stop loss system? If so, how would it operate?
          (b) Recommendations: Does the firm produce a traded options newsletter? If so, is there a charge?
6. Efficiency: Does he appear efficient? When could you expect to receive contract notes and payment for closing positions?
7. Charges: What is the minimum charge (£/%)? Is there a sliding scale of commission charges? Are there special rates for closing or spread transactions?
8. Attitude: What was his attitude towards you?

NINE

BETTING ON TRADED OPTIONS

INTRODUCTION

One of the fastest growth areas in the securities markets over the last five years has been the financial and stock index futures markets. In London, this growth has been championed largely by LIFFE, the London International Financial Futures Exchange, which opened in September 1982 to provide both the domestic and the international market place with a means of protection against adverse movements in interest rates and exchange rates. Over the last few years, this volatility has been greatly magnified by two factors: (a) the increasing globalisation of the securities markets and the profound impact that the US dollar plays on these markets; and (b) multi- and international companies making increasing use of the international Eurodollar and Eurobond markets as an additional way of raising money for further expansion and investment.

Financial and stock index futures were developed initially in the United States to enable investors and corporate institutions with enormous portfolios, such as pension funds, to hedge their investments. These particular futures markets also enable individuals and private investors to take a view on the market themselves and to speculate which way the market as a whole is going. That is, these speculators are people who are prepared to assume price risk and wish to profit from the rise and falls they expect to occur in interest rates or exchange rates. This 'risk' can produce some handsome rewards for the private investor or broker speculating on the futures market, but equally huge losses can be incurred if the market moves sharply in the opposite direction.

As such, the use of options on these markets is a very useful pool not only for the private speculator interested in limiting his potential losses, but also for the professional trader who uses traded options in his day-to-day trading strategy. LIFFE has introduced options on currencies, gilts, US T-bonds, the FT-SE 100 Stock Index future and the short sterling future contract within the last two years, but what is particularly encouraging to see is the increase in options volume, which in total increased by 145 per cent on last year and now represents just under 10 per cent of futures volumes, compared with 7.5 per cent a year ago

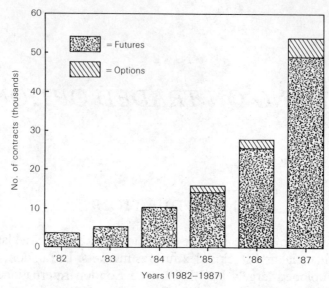

FIG. 9.1 Annual average daily volume of futures and options.
Source: LIFFE.

(see Fig. 9.1 and Table 9.1) – pretty impressive stuff for what is a relatively new market. Nevertheless, by comparison with the traded options on the hugely successful London traded options market, options on futures are still very much the poor relation in terms of turnover, and perhaps also in terms of popularity stakes with the private investor. However, this position is changing. The London Futures and Options Exchange (formally the London Commodity Exchange) introduced options on its coffee, cocoa, sugar and oil contracts only last year – an encouraging sign which shows that traded options are here to stay.

BETTING ON AN OPTION

Why bet on an option instead of buying the option through your broker? The difference here is that the option is based on the futures price and not on the price of the underlying stock. This is a very important distinction, and options on futures should not be confused with the types of options traded on the London traded options market. Whilst both types of options use the same jargon, the fundamental difference is in the cost of the option, or the premium which in turn is influenced by the forward price in the futures market and the underlying share price in the equity market. The already burgeoning market in traded options on commodities and financial futures is growing so rapidly that it may well soon dwarf even the ordinary futures markets. This sensational growth seems fully justified in view of the significant advantages of traded options.

TABLE 9.1 LIFFE: volume for December 1987.

Contract	Volume Dec 87	Volume Nov 87	Per cent change	Volume Dec 86	Per cent change	Jan–Dec 1987	Jan–Dec 1986	Per cent change	Open interest as at 31.12. 87
Futures									
Eurodollar	106,086	146,842	−27.76	66,466	+59.61	1,739,523	1,104,002	+57.57	24,929
Short Sterling	122,249	162,072	−24.57	46,656	+162.02	1,507,920	557,589	+57.47	23,895
US T-Bond	91,191	142,036	−35.80	62,155	+46,72	1,557,360	1,542,331	+0.97	6,053
Long Gilt	362,206	649,889	−44.27	311,917	+16.12	6,995,816	2,612,721	+167.76	19,682
Short Gilt	0	49	−	511	−	235	61,229	−99.62	0
FT-SE 100	40,348	53,754	−24.94	11,963	+237.27	460,615	121,608	+278.77	6,503
JGB[1]	3,486	10,243	−65.97	−	−	133,442	−	−	514
Currencies[2]	363	1,201	−69.78	4,834	−92.49	31,758	71,909	−55.84	304
Total futures	725,929	1,166,086	−37.75	504,502	−43.89	12,426,669	6,471,389	+92.02	81,880
Options									
Short Sterling[3]	6,534	8,283	−21.12	−	−	14,919	−	−	3,212
FT-SE 100	522	109	+378.90	319	+63.64	9,039	2,848	+217.38	60
Dollar-Mark	181	140	+29.29	−	−	2,800	8,286	−66.21	102
Long Gilt	66,077	98,804	−33.12	31,055	+112.72	1,037,306	274,081	+278.47	42,700
Sterling Physical	476	801	−40.57	960	−50.42	15,565	104,329	−85.08	755
Short Eurodollar	1,448	2,362	−38.70	1,814	−20.13	39,866	38,455	+3.67	918
US T-Bond	1,714	3,851	−55.49	2,371	−27.71	54,506	51,790	+5.24	1,609
Total options	76,952	114,350	−32.70	36,519	+110.72	1,174,001	479,789	+144.69	49,356
Total exchange	802,881	1,280,436	−37.30	541,021	+48.40	13,600,670	6,951,278	+95.66	131,236

1. Contract opened: 13 July 1987.
2. Currency futures traded in sterling, Deutschmarks, Swiss francs, yen and dollars. Contract opened 5 November 1987.
Source: LIFFE

TRADED OPTIONS IN THE COMMODITY AND FINANCIAL FUTURES MARKET

In the commodity and financial futures markets, by far the commonest type of option is now the *traded option*. The main characteristic, as the name implies, is that the options themselves are traded. The markets in which dealings on traded options take place lay down what the strike price shall be. For instance, strike prices for options on June Comex gold might range upwards from $400 per ounce at intervals of $20. So the strike prices might be $400, $420, $440 etc., up to $500 per ounce. A private investor or dealer wishing to buy a call option on June gold has to select one of those strike prices. He has the right, upon exercise, to buy a June gold contract at the selected strike price.

The standardisation of the strike prices of traded options is crucial. As there are only a few strike prices available, there will normally be a large group of option holders and grantors at each strike price, or at least at those strike prices which are fairly close to the current level of June gold. So a market will exist in the options at each strike price. The prices of the options, i.e., the premiums paid for them will rise and fall according to supply and demand. Accordingly, a trader in this market is able to get out of a position at any time either by selling an option which he has previously bought, or by buying back one which he has earlier sold.

In principle, betting on futures and options works just the same. The only detailed differences are that in options the deposits are different and the expenses somewhat lower. The big practical difference is that options usually have much bigger moves in price compared to the opening level of the bet and the amount of deposit required. So they normally have bigger percentage moves than the prices of futures. They will not normally move up or down so much in absolute terms, but it is the percentage move which is important. There will be several examples of this later on in the chapter.

Up bets on traded options

The price of a call option tends to rise as the underlying future rises, and, conversely, the price of a put option tends to rise as the price of the future falls. By far the most popular bets are up bets on call options (backing the price of the future to rise) and up bets on put options (backing the price of the future to fall).

Down bets on traded options

While up bets have most of the advantages, clients may certainly make down bets on traded options, if they wish to do so. It should be noted, however, that a down bet on a traded option is simply equivalent to selling a traded option.

A person making a down bet naturally wants the opposite to a person making an up bet: if you make a down bet on a call option, you hope that the price of the underlying contract will fall, while, if you make a down bet on a put option, you hope that the prices of the underlying contract will rise. In either case your maximum possible profit per point is the opening level of your bet (equivalent to the option premium).

The advantages of up bets

While an up bet on a traded option has the obvious disadvantage that, if the price of the underlying future does not move his way, the client may lose the whole price of the option, it has three very important advantages which will now be discussed in detail.

Absolute limit to possible loss

There is no doubt that the biggest appeal of traded options lies in the fact that the possible loss of a client making an up bet is strictly limited. Look at Example 1. (N.B. All examples ignore expenses.)

Example 1

June gold is trading at $444 and the June 440 call options are trading at $21. The client expects gold to rise sharply. He makes a $100 up bet at 21. In fact, gold falls sharply to $400. The option becomes worthless and the bet closes at zero. The client's loss is calculated as follows:

```
 Opening level = 21
  Closing level =  0
    Difference = 21
```

So, the loss on a $100 up bet is 21 × $100 = $2,100.

The client was in no danger of losing more than this whatever happened.

Avoidance of margin calls
Another very important feature of options is that, since the client puts up the maximum amount he can lose (equivalent to the option premium) at the start, he obviously cannot receive any margin call. In a sense this is another way of looking at the limited risk point, but it goes much further than simply giving the client the peace of mind of knowing he cannot lose more than the option premium. He has a different, though related, advantage: he cannot be forced to close out his bet before it expires, no matter how much the price of the underlying contract moves against him. This is illustrated in the following example (2).

Example 2

June Comex gold is trading at $444 and the client expects a sharp fall. He makes a $100 up bet on a 440 put option at 11. A put option gives the right to sell at the strike price and so the price of the option goes up as the price of the corresponding futures price falls.

   To begin with, the price of gold rises sharply so that June Comex gold goes up to $500. The client cannot be called for margin. Then the price goes down to $400 and the client closes his down bet at 40. His profit is calculated as follows:

```
 Closing level = 40
 Opening level = 11
    Difference = 29
```

So, the profit on a $100 up bet is 29 × $100 = $2,900.

The client may well have been unwilling or unable to afford to make a margin payment. If he had made an ordinary bet on the price of June Comex gold, he might have had to close it out at a considerable loss when the price went up to $500. Because he had bet on an option he avoided that problem and came out with an excellent profit.

Gearing

The holder of an option gets favourable 'gearing'. Gearing is the relationship between the possible profit and possible loss in any transaction. We know that the client in Example 1 was safer in the knowledge that he could not lose more than $2,100. The importance of high gearing, however, goes far beyond the mere comfort of knowing that you can only lose a little but may make a lot – important though this may be. It means that a buyer of an option, or a client with an up bet, may well, if prices move his way, be able to make many times what he could have made for the same outlay if he had entered into a normal futures contract.

Example 3

This is an example of an up bet on an FT-SE call option. On 20 August 1987 when the actual FT-SE Index was about 2,185 and IG's quote for the September FT-SE was about 2,185–2,192, a client asked what the price would be for an up bet in a September FT-SE 2,200 call option. He was told it would be 44 and he decided to open a £5 up bet. His maximum possible loss was 44 × £5 = £220. On 30 September, when FT-SE settled at 2,363, his option was closed out at 163. His profit was calculated as follows:

Closing level = 163
Opening level = 44
Difference = 119

So, the profit on a £5 up bet is 119 × £5 = £595, a return of 170 per cent.

Remember that the client in the above example (which is a real one) could not lose more than £220 whatever happened, but in fact he more than doubled his investment and made a profit of £595, in just five weeks. This shows one advantage of favourable gearing.

But there is another very important point. If he could afford no more than the £220 which he had to put up as a deposit for his option bet, he would not have been able to afford an ordinary £5 up bet on the March FT-SE at, say, 1,766 because the deposit would have been nearly £500.

Another important point about gearing is that a client making a bet on a cheaper option will get more gearing than one betting on a more expensive option.

Example 4

June gold is trading at $444 and two clients expect a sharp rise. Each of them can afford to lose $2,000.

Client A decides to make a $100 up bet on the 440 June Comex gold option at 21. The price of gold increases sharply to $550 just before the option expires. The option is trading by then at 110 and so his profit is calculated as follows:

Closing level = 110
Opening level = 21
Difference = 89

So, the profit on a $100 up bet is 89 × $100 = $8,900.

Client B decides to make a $500 up bet on the 480 Comex gold option at 4. At the point when Client A closes his bet at 110, i.e., when June gold is trading at 550, the call option is worth 70. So Client B closes his at 70. His profit is calculated as follows:

Closing level = 70
Opening level = 4
Difference = 66

So, the profit on a $500 up bet is 66 × $500 = $33,000.

Client B's profit per dollar bet was, as you can see, less than the profit per dollar bet of Client A (66 against 89) because the price of his option moved up a smaller number of points. However, because the amount he had to put up as deposit (equal to his maximum possible loss) was so much less per dollar bet (4 against 21) he was able to make a much bigger bet and so his total profit was considerably more than that of Client A. This again shows the potential advantages of gearing.

BETTING ON STOCK MARKET OPTIONS

One of the most popular kinds of option bet is a bet on a stock market option. This popularity is well deserved because large profits can be made without taking any risk of large losses, as illustrated in Example 4, where the client's maximum possible loss was £570, but he actually made a profit of £1,270.

It is vitally important, however, to realise that a stock index option is not an option on the current level of the stock index but on its level for a future date. So the movement of the price of the option will depend on how the stock index *futures* move, which is not by any means necessarily the same thing as the way the actual level of the index itself moves. This can prove to be a great advantage for the client or a great disadvantage, and we shall give one example of each. Broadly speaking, it will prove an advantage if the client's views are different from those of most people, but a disadvantage if they are the same. It is certainly vital, if the client is to avoid possible disappointment, that he understands the point.

It is also important to realise that, in spite of the high gearing which options often have, a call option never actually moves up more, in absolute terms, than the price of the underlying contract. However, the percentage move for the option will always, provided the move takes place rapidly, be greater than the percentage move of the underlying contract.

Example 5

On 2 March the current level of the FT-SE Index is 1,755. Most people expect it to fall and the March futures price (ignoring spreads, as throughout this section) is 1,745. The client disagrees with the opinion of the majority and expects the market to rise. He finds that March 1,750 call options are trading at 15 and he opens a £10 up bet at 15. Two days later he finds the market has moved up just 10 points to 1,765, but the majority of people now expect the market to rise further and the March futures price is 1,775. The price of the March 1,750 call option has moved up in the wake of the sharp increase in the level of the futures, and now stands at 25. The client decides to take his profit and closes his bet at 25. His profit is calculated as follows:

     Closing level = 25
     Opening level = 15
       Difference = 10

So, the profit on a £10 up bet is 10 × £10 = £100.

The client in Example 5 made a profit of nearly 70 per cent, even though the actual level of the FT-SE Index did not move very much. But look at Example 6, which shows the other side of the coin.

Example 6

On 15 June the current level of the FT-SE Index is 1,849. Most people expect it to rise and the December futures price is 1,870. The client also expects the market to rise. He finds that the December 1,850 call options are trading at 37, and he opens a £10 up bet at 37. Two days later the market has risen 10 points to 1,859 but most people are now much less optimistic and the December futures price is trading at 1,858. The price of the December 1,850 call option has *fallen*, in spite of the rise in the actual level of the FT-SE Index, because the December futures price has fallen. The call option how stands at 31 and the client closes his bet. The client has made a loss, which is calculated as follows:

Opening level = 37
Closing level = 31
Difference = 6

So, the loss on a £20 up bet is 6 × £10 = £60.

It is important for the investor to realise that the kind of disappointment illustrated in Example 6 can happen. One way to recognise the danger is to ask, when deciding whether to open a bet, not only the price of the option you are interested in, but also the price of the underlying future. If the price of the future is substantially above the actual level of the FT-SE Index, the option will be reflecting that optimism. You have to realise that, if you want to close your bet when that optimism is no longer there, the price of the future, and therefore also that of the call option, may be disappointingly low.

HOW TO MAKE A PROFIT

You may feel you have had to do a lot of reading to get to the point where you are told what you really want to know, i.e., under what circumstances it is possible to make money out of up bets on traded options!

For simplicity we will assume that the option is a call option – obviously, prices need to move the other way for a put option. Basically, a client with an up bet on a call option will make money if either of the following happens:

1. The price of the underlying contract moves up, before the option expires, to a point where it is above the strike price by more than the opening level of your bet. If you opened an up bet at 20 on a June 440 Comex gold call option, for instance, you would be able to close it for more than 20 if June Comex gold went above 460. A client's long-term break-even level for a call option is, therefore, strike price plus opening level (for a put option – strike price minus opening level).

2. You can also make money if the price of the underlying contract rises rapidly – and it is not necessary that it should be above the strike price. Suppose, for instance, a client opens an up bet in March on a June 480 Comex gold call option at a price of four when June gold is trading at 450. If gold has a sharp rise so that June gold is trading the next day at 470, he will certainly see the price of the option rise. After all, from the point of view of a seller of a 480 call option the danger of the price of June gold going above 480 is now much higher than before the $20 move, so that the option may well now be trading

TABLE 9.2 June Comex gold
call options: March.

Strike price	Option price
400	42
420	26
440	14
460	7
480	3

at 9, giving you a profit of 5, i.e. over 100 per cent, even though the futures price is still below both the strike price and below the long-term break-even level of 480 + 4, i.e. 484. The option has no intrinsic value – indeed it may never have any intrinsic value. Yet the holder can still take a good profit.

You may want to know how much of a move the option is likely to have if there is a quick $20 rise in the price of June gold. You can get a good idea by looking at the price of some options with different strike prices. Table 9.2 shows a list of prices of June Comex gold call options in March when June gold was trading at $440.

From this table you can see that when June gold was $440 an option with a strike price of 20 above that, i.e. a 460 call option, was trading at seven. So it is likely that if gold had a rapid $20 rise to 460, the 480 call option, which would have a strike price 20 above the current level of June gold, would also be trading at 7. So you can expect that a $20 rise from $440 to $460 in the price of June gold will be reflected by a move from $3 to approximately $7 (57 per cent) in the price of a 460 call option.

This gives only a rough guide and you certainly have to remember that we are dealing with a very rapid price movement in the underlying contract. If a significant amount of time has elapsed then the move will be less because there will naturally be a loss of time value.

TEN

THE USE OF COMPUTERS
IN TRADED OPTIONS
AND TECHNICAL ANALYSIS

INTRODUCTION

The concepts involved in the use of traded options for improving investment returns and the employment of technical analysis techniques in determining probable stock price movements are relatively simple. The mathematics involved in these techniques, however, is often highly complicated.

The calculation of a theoretical fair price for a traded option using the traditional Black–Scholes valuation model using a pocket calculator (see Chapter Seven) is by no means impossible for the investor with a good knowledge of mathematics. But, in practice, the calculations are very time consuming and prone to error. The estimation of the fair value for an option using a more complex and accurate formula, such as the Binomial model, might take the average investor with a good knowledge of mathematics many hours to perform. In a fast moving market, the manual calculation of option prices to determine whether an option is over- or under-priced becomes totally impractical. By the time the investor is in a position to make a judgment, the option price is likely to have moved, requiring a further set of calculations to be made.

The mathematics involved in calculating technical analysis indicators is less arduous but still impractical for the investor wishing to study a wide range of companies on a day-to-day basis. For the computer, however, all these tasks are a simple matter and a manual calculation which takes hours can be performed by everyday home computers in fractions of a second. For the serious option trader, the calculation speed and the practicality of using computers are essential pre-requisites to successful trading.

On occasion, both computers and traded options have received some blame for accentuating volatile movements in the market and even for the crash of 19 October 1987. There have also been calls for controls on the use of traded options and futures, but these would almost certainly hinder the implementation of sensible risk management as practised by professional fund managers. Without this hedging capability, the market would be a far more nervous environment for all participants.

In some cases, criticism of the use of computers has been fair but in others, totally misplaced. Even in cases where computers have contributed to market volatility this has often been due to fast electronic 'number-crunchers' determining and taking advantage of anomalies in the market. The World's financial markets never cease to trade in different countries, currencies and with a host of complex financial instruments. The complexities are of such a high order that the human mind and pocket calculator cannot operate fast enough to smooth out all anomalies. If a computer program can determine that to buy a commodity in one part of the World and sell immediately in another will give a profit, then the owner of the program has gained a considerable advantage over the investor who is unaware of the imbalance. Although it can be argued that in certain cases computers can generate more volatility in the financial markets, it is unlikely that their owners will have much to complain about. It is the latter's intention to be first in the queue for buying at the bottom and selling at the top, and the growing sophistication of computer software is likely to give the computer user an edge over the investor who rejects such assistance.

The advantages to the investor of using a computer as an investment aid are many and include the following:

1. The computer can perform many thousands of calculation-intensive procedures in seconds, leaving the investor free to employ his judgment in terms of how or when to trade.
2. The computer's great speed allows the investor vastly to increase the range of techniques used in his decision-making.
3. Huge amounts of information can be analysed, assimilated and stored by the computer for instant recall in the future.
4. The probability of errors or mistakes, which can be critical in investment decisions, is enormously reduced.
5. Modern technology and communications can be utilised by the computer to provide automated price retrieval and open an 'electronic window' into the World's financial markets.

The disadvantage of using computers is simply one of price and the natural fear shared by so many unfamiliar with the nature and use of these remarkable devices. A few years ago, a powerful computer would have cost the investor many thousands of pounds, and specialist computer software designed to provide the trader with evaluative investment tools would often cost even more. The dramatic increase in computer power coupled with falling costs and readily available investment software now means that the investor can acquire a complete system for under a thousand pounds. Any serious trader who dismisses the benefits of computers on the grounds of cost is likely to pay a heavy price, as he will surely fall behind the growing band of traders who have come to appreciate their value.

Using a modern, low cost, desktop computer and a communications link to a share price database, the investor can, in the space of a few minutes, do the following:

1. Update his share price files automatically via the modem and telephone lines.
2. Extract the latest bid and offer prices for each traded option.
3. Conduct a technical analysis study on the underlying share price histories, looking for buying opportunities or to determine an 'outlook' for the market.
4. Analyse the option premiums, looking for the most favourably priced options.
5. Determine possible strategies which may be suitable in view of his projection for future share prices and his personal investment aims.
6. Assess the likely profitability of the trade, if expectations are met, or potential losses should the share price move against the expected trend.

In a short period of time, the computer will have performed thousands of calculations and accomplished many repetitive and time-consuming tasks. As pointed out above, the computer has given the trader the ability to assimilate and analyse the information available electronically, leaving him to make the final judgment on which companies to trade. In consequence, the investor who relies on instinct or manual calculations trades at a distinct disadvantage to the modern computerised trader.

CHOICE OF HARDWARE AND SOFTWARE

The investor or trader who wishes to take advantage of computer technology has some important decisions to make: what hardware to purchase in terms of the computer itself, which peripheral devices, such as printer, and, just as important, which criteria he needs to employ in choosing the best software to perform the desired task.

For those who have no knowledge of computing, the computer is a high speed processing and calculating machine but in itself cannot provide the tools to help improve investment performance. This function is performed by the software which has been specifically designed to utilise the high speed calculation potential of the computer and provide the user with the means of entering instructions in a form which the trader understands, while translating those commands into a form that the computer can process.

The electronics industry has spawned a bewildering array of machines and peripheral hardware, all with their own unique array of features and facilities and different specifications for speed and power. The technology of computers is a fast-moving target and many potential purchasers are always concerned that today's state-of-the-art machine will be obsolete tomorrow. One standard, however, which has become universal in the business computing world is that set by IBM with the release of its IBM PC computer. Many manufacturers now produce computers which are compatible with this standard. Improvements in technology have resulted in considerable increases in speed and capacity for this standard of machine, ensuring that it will enjoy a long lifetime before becoming obsolete. The ubiquity of the IBM PC standard has resulted in every serious software house striving to ensure that their programs will be compatible with the IBM PC and related computers. As a result, the worldwide investment in this standard will ensure that the owner of such a machine will have access to new computer software which will operate with this hardware into the foreseeable future.

The IBM standard has been emulated by many computer manufacturers, such as Compaq, Olivetti, Toshiba, Amstrad and a host of others. Although the basic nature of these different IBM-compatible machines is the same, their speed, power and cost can vary enormously. For £500 or so, the investor can purchase an Amstrad PC-compatible computer with twin disk drive which will give all the facilities of a traditional IBM PC computer, but at a fraction of the price. For a thousand pounds more, a higher speed machine with an internal hard disk allowing high speed, high capacity storage can be acquired. Essentially, the higher cost computers provide high capacity, internal, hard disks and faster processing speeds, whereas the lower cost computers tend to be slower machines with lower capacity, floppy disk storage systems. Additional hardware, such as plug-in hard disks and higher resolution graphics monitors, can be added to the more basic IBM-compatible machines, ensuring that the user can start at a relatively low cost base and build up his system at a later time. The investor who purchases a low entry level computer will normally, however, be tied to a specific processor's speed which cannot easily be upgraded to provide faster calculation times.

The choice of which computer to purchase involves deciding on the following:

1. The type of basic computer.
2. The file storage system.
3. The graphics capability.

Basic computer system

This should be determined by the amount you are willing to pay and the speed and type of the computer's internal processor. The latter will govern which generation of PC you will be acquiring.

The choice of processor determines how quickly the computer will be able to perform calculations and process information. Processors basically fall into three categories as follows:

1. 8086/8088 processors: These are the equivalent to that fitted on the IBM/PC computer and represent the first generation PC and the lowest level of IBM computing. Some manufacturers have increased the basic operating speed of this type of processor with the result that they can operate two or three times faster than the equivalent IBM PC computer.
2. 80286 processor: This is the processor fitted to the second generation IBM AT computer and is substantially quicker than the 8086 processor. Once again, other manufacturers have accelerated the processing speed of the 80286 processor, resulting in increased performance.
3. 80386 processor: This is the latest generation of processors fitted to the IBM compatible range of computers and represents a further significant increase over the speed of the 80286 processor.

In practical terms, the later generation of processors do represent quite dramatic increases in speed over the early 8086/8088 versions. A task which might be performed in ten seconds on an 8086-based machine can be performed in the blink of an eye on an 80386-based machine. The costs of acquiring these more sophisticated models do, however, rise dramatically. The 8086- or 8088-based machines usually cost under £1,000, with 80286-based machines approaching the £2,000 barrier. The cost of the more advanced 80386 machines is now starting to fall but is likely to be several thousand pounds.

Apart from the processor and its accompanying electronics, the basic hardware of the three generations of computers is broadly the same. The difference between a cheap IBM clone and the original IBM PC computer is usually one of robustness and reliability, although the current generation of machines rarely show problems of reliability. The cheaper machines do not, however, carry the same amount of servicing and support available with the more expensive machines in the same class but sometimes out-perform them in terms of speed.

The investor who is looking for a budget machine would probably prefer to choose a low cost 8086- or 8088-based computer whereas the investor with a little more to spend, who wishes to gain a major improvement in speed, will opt for the more potent 80286-based machine.

Choice of disk storage system

IBM-compatible computers can be purchased with three alternatives of disk storage system as follows:

1. Single floppy drive machines. These are not recommended for use with serious computer software as the majority of software packages require the

use of one drive which holds the software program disk and a second drive to hold the disk which is used for storing data. Although single drive computers can treat the one drive as if it were two, frequent disk changes are often required, making this variant of machine impractical in day-to-day use.

2. Twin floppy drive machines. These are the recommended minimum specification for investors requiring a serious computer at a budget price. They should support the majority of investment software but will present speed and capacity limitations in terms of assessing data files when compared with hard disk versions. Floppy disk systems can be subsequently upgraded to hard disk systems without difficulty.

To further complicate matters, floppy disk systems are normally designed to accommodate the traditional 5.25-inch disks which have the capacity to store 360,000 characters of information. Some machines now support the later 3.5-inch disks which are more robust and have an increased capacity to store 720,000 characters of data. The 3.5-inch disk is likely to become the floppy disk standard of the future but is incorporated into few PC-compatible machines at the present time. Not all software houses support this type of disk, so, before buying a machine fitted with a 3.5 inch drive, it is worth checking that the software you wish to purchase can be supplied in this format.

3. Hard disk versions. These have an internal high speed, high capacity disk with sufficient space to store the equivalent amount of data of between 30 and over 100 standard floppy disks. This type of disk drive has many advantages in terms of convenience over floppy disk systems. Hard disk systems can be purchased with as low as ten megabyte capacity (i.e. to hold ten million characters of information) ranging up to 40 megabytes or more. In practice, however, the operating system of the computer can usually only utilise at any one time approximately 30 megabytes of hard disk space and the most popular size of hard disk purchased is a 20 megabyte hard disk which has the equivalent capacity of sixty 5.25-inch floppy disks. In the case of many software programs, the operating program, together with the data are stored within the hard disk, ensuring that your program can be run and data files accessed many times faster than on any equivalent floppy disk system.

Graphics capability

The majority of IBM-compatible computers can be fitted with four basic types of displays, as follows:

1. Text only. This usually relates to monochrome machines which do not have any kind of graphics card fitted. Only the display of text is possible, and

charts cannot be produced without the installation of an additional graphics card.

2. Hercules graphics cards. These were designed to give a graphics capability to the early text-only IBM machines, but are still fitted to some computers supplied with monochrome monitors and no alternative graphics card. Not all graphics software will operate with these cards and a potential purchaser of a computer supplied with a monochrome monitor is advised to check with his supplier whether a Hercules or Hercules-compatible card has been installed. If this is the case, then he should ensure that the software he intends to purchase has been designed to operate with this type of card.

3. Colour graphics adaptor (CGA) card. This is the basic graphics adaptor installed in computers fitted with a colour monitor. Some manufacturers, such as Compaq, Olivetti and Amstrad, have designed special hardware which allows the facilities of a colour graphics adaptor to be used on a computer operating with a monochrome monitor. Virtually all software which can produce graphics is likely to operate with this type of graphics card, although the CGA card is unable to produce colour with high resolution charts.

4. Enhanced graphics adaptor (EGA) card. The EGA card is a more sophisticated version of the CGA card and supports higher resolution graphics with colour. For investors wishing to utilise charts, this is the ideal type of card to purchase, as high definition colour charts will be possible. Most computers can be upgraded to contain a more advanced type of graphics card, although this is not the case with the popular Amstrad PC1512 machine.

Memory requirement

The memory of the computer determines the size of the program that it can run and the amount of data which can be stored internally (for rapid manipulation) at any point in time. The majority of computers are fitted with 512K or 640K of memory which should be sufficient for runniing your preferred investment software package. Some computers can be purchased with lower amounts of installed memory, but 512K is the recommended minimum if you plan to run the more sophisticated software. It is quite a simple matter and relatively inexpensive to upgrade IBM-compatible computer to 512K, or even the effective maximum of 640K, and your dealer should be able to carry out this work in a few minute.

In summary, therefore, the investor who wishes to acquire an IBM-compatible computer needs to make his choice of which base processing unit he requires, and then whether it is fitted with a hard or floppy disk system and to what extent he wishes to utilise high resolution graphics for charting purposes.

A computer fitted with an internal hard disk and enhanced graphics card provides all that the investor could require and any additional expense would involve the purchase of later generation machines with a faster internal processor.

Peripheral equipment

Once the basic computer system has been acquired, the investor will require a printer and possibly a modem for communicating with outside data sources. A relatively inexpensive printer, such as an Epson-compatible dot matrix printer, would give high performance, high speed printing and a graphics capability with most investment software.

Additional expense on printers will usually result in higher speed and quality of the printed text and if typewriter quality text is required, then a daisy wheel printer should be considered. A daisy wheel printer will not, however, be capable of reproducing screen graphics, and is usually confined to computer users who require a high quality word-processing capability.

Choice of software

Once the investor has acquired an acceptable choice of computer hardware, he is then faced with the difficult task of obtaining the software package which will meet his requirements. Irrespective of the speed and power of the computer equipment, software is the bridge between the user and his machine. The quality of software can vary enormously; a badly designed program can make poor use of the computer's facilities, can prove difficult to use the produce less than ideal results. A well-designed piece of software can be a pleasure to use and can transform a simple request from the investor into meaningful and well-presented results with a minimum of effort.

The requirements of the investor are very diverse and it is very likely that any single piece of software will perform all the required functions. This will probably apply whether the software costs a few hundred or a few thousand pounds.

Before making his choice of software, the investor should seek detailed information on the performance and facilities of each package under consideration and should satisfy himself that the software is easy to use and performs the desired tasks. Many investors, having spent a thousand pounds or more on a computer, decide to save money on the choice of software by buying the cheapest computer program available. This is invariably a false economy as the software is the vehicle with which the investor will be working, with the computer simply providing the environment within which the software operates.

In the case of computers and investment software, it is far better to buy a good package and cheap computer than a high quality computer and poorly designed software package. The investor should, therefore, be looking for software which is good value, easy to use, well designed and provides as many facilities as are regarded essential and desirable by its potential user.

THE USE OF TECHNICAL ANALYSIS

As explained in Chapter Four, technical analysis, in its simplest form, is chart pattern analysis. The technical analyst attempts to determine from the behaviour of prices in the past an insight into where the prices will move in the future. The simplest forms of technical analysis involve looking for particular chart patterns such as 'head and shoulders' configurations, 'rounded tops and bottoms' and particular items such as 'flags' and 'pennants'. Paradoxically, this is one area of technical analysis that computers are not suited for. The 'head and shoulders' pattern is, for example, characterised by a sequence of three peaks, the middle peak being higher than the other two. The human eye can detect this without too much difficulty but this involves a degree of judgment, as the slopes on the peaks may vary, the entire formation may take place over a matter of weeks or months and the period of time between the first and second peaks may be totally different to that between the second and third peaks.

Any computer program revolves around a set of rules established by the programmer. In the case of a simple chart configuration, such as the 'head and shoulders' pattern, the mathematical rules are almost impossibly complex. This is why technical analysis is often referred to as an art rather than a science, but, as with all arts, good tools are required to do the job well. This is especially true for technical analysis. The computer is the tool which gives the trader time to think and act on the information that the computer provides. In the first place, it can produce in seconds a chart of the share price history, which will allow the investor to determine and to see the 'head and shoulders' pattern or any other technical analysis configuration which indicates a probable market move in a specific direction.

The majority of investment trading rules revolve around pure mathematical indicators such as moving averages, overbought/oversold indicators, relative strength, etc. In this area, the computer stands supreme, as each of these indicators requires the performance of a number of well-defined mathematical calculations and the immediate translation of the results of these calculations on to the computer monitor screen. Almost every conceivable technical analysis indicator, with the exception of pure chart patterns, involves the application of a set of mathematical rules to the raw share price data. The moving average is the simplest form of indicator, but more complex ones, such as the Stochastic process, can be handled by computers with equal ease.

The chartist who completes his charts manually and performs his calculations by hand plots the latest points for each indicator, but his decision-making process may be thrown by chart errors and the sheer waste of effort in maintaining hundreds of charts. He will be side-tracked from his prime objective, which is to spot buying and selling opportunities. A good computer charting program should provide facilities for selecting moving averages, oscillators and other technical indicators with total flexibility, and should also provide the ability to view critical areas of the chart in great detail.

When choosing a software package, the chartist should be looking for software which can draw at least two moving averages with the average period totally selectable by the user (see Chapter Four). The calculation of moving averages is difficult and time-consuming and the manual chartist cannot experiment with alternative average systems without needing to re-draw charts from scratch. The computer chartist can experiment as much as he likes in the knowledge that any variation will be drawn by the computer in seconds giving a much greater insight into the share being studied.

One of the most popular trading indicators is the overbought/oversold indicator, the rate of change oscillator (ROC) (see Glossary). When the price is rising rapidly the share is said to be overbought and nearing the point when the movement of sellers into the market will cause the price to stabilise and then fall. When the share price is following rapidly and nearing its trough the share is said to be oversold and nearing a point when a reversal is likely. The overbought/oversold indicator is an invaluable trading tool, particularly when studying shares which fluctuate between pronounced peaks and troughs. The computer will usually represent this as an undulating curve which oscillates around a value of 50 and can peak as high as 100, or fall as low as zero on the overbought/oversold scale. The share is normally considered overbought and ripe for profit-taking when the curve rises above a value of 80 or oversold, and worth a buy, when the curve falls below the 20 level. This indicator can also be used as a confirmatory indicator. If the share price achieves a new high which is not confirmed by a peak in this indicator then the price high should be treated with suspicion. The signals generated by this indicator can be uncannily accurate and the overbought/oversold indicator should be an essential facility in any good technical analysis program.

One other key indicator for the short-term trader is the stochastic process which is a combined moving average and overbought/oversold indicator (see Chapter Four again for a fuller explanation). This indicator is normally only available in the more sophisticated software packages but is an excellent aid for predicting short-term reversals.

Point and figure charts are a more specialised technical analysis tool primarily designed to concentrate the major trading moves into a sequence of chart patterns, while dispensing with the 'noise' associated with short-term moves of little consequence. Unlike line charts, the x-axis scale of point and figure charts does not represent time in a strict sense. These charts are mainly used to identify areas of accumulation (buying) and distribution (selling) and give a picture of supply and demand. A point and figure chart can produce many buying and selling signals and can highlight well-defined trends and chart patterns, such as 'flags' and 'pennants'.

The more sophisticated investor who has access to daily high/low and close information and also the volume of trading in each stock or commodity can gain an insight into the strength or weakness of market moves using daily bar charts, volume charts and breadth indicators such as the advance/decline line. The use of volume in technical analysis is an important factor in investment timing and gives a more complete picture of the driving force behind share price movements. The factors which affect the movement of the share price are principally ones of demand and supply. If more buyers are in the market than sellers then the price is likely to rise and the reverse applies when sellers exceed buyers. However, the market-makers can alter the price of a share in order to stimulate demand in any particular direction and true investor sentiment might not, therefore, be contained in a particular short-term share price move. Volume analysis will assist considerably in highlighting what is really occurring in the market place.

One other feature which is important in a good technical analysis package is the ability to draw trend lines (see Chapter Four again for a full explanation of these). The drawing of these lines requires a degree of human visual judgment and needs to be carried out by moving the lines into position manually on the computer.

The technical analyst will find any one of the indicators from this arsenal of tools of use in isolation, but if the computer program provides facilities to place them all on the screen at the same time, then the investor will be able to look for corroboration between the various indicators to improve the probability of his judgment being correct.

In summary, these technical indicators form the toolkit which the trader employs to detect opportunities and optimise timing. Without such techniques as his disposal, he would need to rely on instinct and the market fundamentals such as yields and PE ratios. In today's volatile international markets, these techniques are used by an increasing number of successful traders. The trader who ignores such techniques does so at his peril.

TRADED OPTIONS ANALYSIS

The analysis of traded options using manual techniques is a formidable task and quite beyond the mathematical capability of the majority of investors. In this field, the computer excels and should be employed by anyone with a serious involvement in trading options.

The actual premium quoted for a call or put option is based on the application of quite complex mathematical formulae which take account of all the variables that would affect the probability of making or losing money on the option. These include the volatility of the share price itself, i.e. the likelihood of the underlying share price moving within a specific range up or down within a given time period. The time to expiry also has an important part to play, as the longer the time remaining before maturity, the more time is available for a significant upswing or downswing in the market to result in profits or losses for the purchaser of the option. Even items such as the current risk-free interest rate are of importance because the investor who wishes to purchase an option always has the alternative of placing his funds with total safety in the bank or building society. The current underlying share price also has a major part to play, as the price of the option will vary depending upon whether it is in-the-money, at-the-money or out-of-the-money.

Only a computer program is well placed to take all of these factors into account, and to determine the theoretical fair premium that should apply to any given option at any point in time prior to maturity. Many formulae have been suggested for the pricing of options, but computer programs which have been designed to calculate the fair price of an option commonly employ the Black–Scholes model (see Chapter Seven). Although this model was developed as far back as 1973, to coincide with the opening of trading on the Chicago Board options exchange, it is still the best known valuation model. Despite its popularity, however, the Black–Scholes model is deficient in a number of ways: in particular, in that it does not strictly apply to the American style of options traded in London. That is to say, the model does not take into account the fact the American options can be exercised before maturity and hence sometimes can be worth more 'dead' (exercised) than 'alive' (unexercised). For call options, the decision to exercise will only be optimal just prior to the ex-dividend date. Although some modifications can be made to the Black–Scholes model to adjust for the incidence of dividends, and even early exercise, there are certain circumstances where the Black–Scholes model will over or undervalue an option premium.

A more sophisticated pricing method uses the Binomial model originally derived by William Sharpe and later developed by Cox–Ross–Rubenstein. This attempts to overcome the deficiencies of the Black–Scholes model. The Binomial method is, however, very calculation-intensive due to the fact that it is a discrete model as opposed to the limiting case of the continuous Black–Scholes model. But herein lies its advantage because it enables proper adjustment for dividends, early exercise and also alternative types of stock price movements. To utilise this model, the computer is of paramount importance. The investor using manual techniques would need to perform many thousands of calculations in order to value one option price.

A good options package should provide the investor with the facility to employ either technique in order to determine whether an option has been fairly priced. In recent years, a number of other models have been formulated in order to calculate the fair price of an opinion and some software packages might use these different techniques in their calculation processes.

When using an option analysis package, the investor is normally trying to identify options which are mispriced. A mispriced option can be over- or under-priced, and an analysis of all the option premiums for a particular company bearing in mind the different strike prices and expiry dates will reveal anomalies in the pricing. The trader who wishes to take up an option position must be aware of these anomalies in order to determine whether the option in which he would like to trade is over-priced, fairly priced, or apparently cheap, based on current market conditions.

When an option trader has gained a deeper understanding of the nature of option pricing he is likely to want to investigate the use of more sophisticated techniques. These include strategies which are a combination of two or more option positions in the same security in order to capitalise on his expectations for the movements in the underlying share price. A strategy can be designed to make money if the share price moves up, down, or outside a given range. Alternatively, it can be designed to make money if the share price moves within a given range or remains totally static. Basically, any outlook for the market can be catered for by an option strategy.

A good options analysis program should be capable of reproducing charts and providing the user with the freedom to create any strategy of his choice and view its expected outcome. In addition, some allowance ought to be made for the commission on each individual option transaction, both on the purchase and the sale, as these can significantly alter the profit prospects of a particular strategy. For example, a butterfly spread very often looks attractive when viewed without taking dealing costs into account. When you remember that this strategy involves four options, the dealing costs involved can make the trade look less profitable.

Ideally, the profit prospect of the strategy at any point in time prior to maturity of the first leg of the strategy should be represented so that the investor can determine the effects of a short-term movement in the underlying share price. In graphical form, this representation is called the 'premium delta curve' (see Chapter Seven again) and is performed by calculating the fair value of the combined option position at a number of different underlying share prices as at the chosen point in time. This produces a curve where the investor can read off the probable profit at any selected date, for any underlying share price. The premium delta curve, because of its difficulty of calculation, is not always shown on stylised graphical representations of strategies in books but is nevertheless an essential feature in a computer software program designed for option analysis.

One useful, but not always present, facility is the ability to chart the effect of movements in the option price following a change in any particular key factor such as interest rate or time. This will give the investor an insight, for example, into the effect on an option price of an increase or decrease in the volatility. It will also give a greater understanding of the nature of option pricing and the best techniques to use in order to maximise profits and reduce risk.

The use of software for analysing options is of immense value in improving the prospects of making profits and reducing risks, but these benefits can be accentuated if combined with the technical analysis ability that can help pinpoint the time when the share price is likely to move in favour of the investor. After all, it is share price movements which affect the performance of the option. Ideally, a software package which can handle both aspects will be of most value. The following section discusses the use of one such package, illustrating the benefits that can be obtained with the help of this type of computer software.

USING A TYPICAL OPTIONS ANALYSIS PACKAGE

In the UK, the choice of software packages designed for traded options is limited, except in the case of professional back office systems costing thousands of pounds.

One of the best budget packages designed for the small investor is the OptionMaster Plus package from Synergy Software, which retails, at the time of writing, for £300. This is a combined options analysis and technical analysis package designed for the IBM PC and compatible machines with a minimum memory of 512K. Synergy also produce OptionMaster which covers options analysis only and retails for £150.

Essentially, the options analysis and technical analysis aspects of the package have been integrated into an easy-to-use and flexible environment which allows the user to study complex strategies and then, in seconds, chart the share price history, using a combination of moving averages, overbought/oversold oscillators and other important predictive indicators.

OptionMaster's 'valuation screen' allows you to enter all the details of an option, such as the volatility, underlying price, etc., and then produces an instant valuation of the option using the Black–Scholes or Cox–Ross–Rubenstein valuation models. Commodities and futures are also catered for. If an actual option premium is entered, then the implied volatility will also be displayed. The price history files which are used for technical analysis purposes are automatically read by OptionMaster to determine the historic volatility of the share price history for any chosen number of days. This means that all the essential items of option valuation are available on one screen with any item being easily amended and the new value calculated.

When experimenting with some of the American packages, it is often necessary to enter all the details of an option before a valuation can be performed. OptionMaster can store any existing option transactions and load them into its valuation or strategy screens. This allows an investor to view and value his position immediately.

The strategy analysis screen is a little more complex but extracts all existing options found in the program's database for the chosen security. The investor can immediately value the strategy or conduct a simulation up to its maturity. Individual legs can be removed or new legs can be added quite simply, enabling the investor to experiment with different strategies or even invent new ones.

The most valuable facility of OptionMaster is its ability to chart the profit profile of single options or complex strategies, allowing the investor to reproduce textbook strategy charts in seconds. Premium delta curves are also drawn which enable the expected profits at any point in time to be read off the scale on the chart.

The option valuation screen gives the following useful statistics which help in choosing a particular option:

1. Delta. This is a measure in the change of the option price for a smallest movement in the underlying security price and gives an idea of the likely acceleration in option price should the share price increase.
2. Gamma. This is a measure of the rate of change of the delta for a small change in the stock price and is a useful indicator for investors who wish to hedge stock positions with equivalent contrary option positions.
3. The elasticity. This is a percentage representation of how a small percentage change in the underlying security will affect the option premium. A high elasticity will lead to a more volatile option price but nevertheless quick profits if a move takes place in the desired direction.

Although the delta is a common statistic in option packages, the premium delta curve which the OptionMaster package produces allows you to see just how rapidly the option premium moves in relation to a rise or fall in the share price.

The charting aspect of this package is of value to investors who are attempting to understand the traded options market and provides a variety of specialist charts on the various factors which affect option premiums. It is possible to select, for example, a chart of changes in option premium based on interest rates, underlying share price or dividend yield allowing a complete simulation of the behaviour of an option under different market conditions.

The technical analysis features are comprehensive and easy-to-use and include point and figure charts, moving averages, oscillators, relative strength and stochastics in addition to a handful of other indicators. The comparison facilities are also very flexible, allowing multiple lines to be displayed on the same screen. The technical analysis module employs a useful memory technique where the same indicators can be re-drawn on each chart automatically. This allows all the UK traded option price histories to be analysed, using moving average and overbought/oversold indicators, in a few minutes.

The mathematical models used allow for the instance of dividends on a continuous yield basis which, in the case of the Black–Scholes model, gives a more accurate result than the traditional method. The Cox–Ross–Rubenstein model is slow in comparison but produces a higher order of accuracy.

Although options analysis and technical analysis programs are relatively commonplace in America, they tend to lean substantially to that market. As a result they are often difficult to apply in the UK market.

SUMMARY

In summary, the investor who wishes to take full advantage of the profit possibilities of the traded options market should regard a computer as an essential piece of equipment. Without it he will need to rely on guesswork and instinct in a market where mathematics and probabilities are the order of the day.

Prospective developments in information technology and communications will make it even more essential that the trader should computerise his trading activities. The investor who shuns this technology in favour of older methods will almost certainly be at a disadvantage to the traders who have taken the plunge. The demand in traded options and other high leverage instruments is accelerating and is a worldwide phenomenon unlikely to abate. As these complex instruments grow in importance, more and more sophisticated techniques will be devised to improve the chances of the investor. In the investment world, the computer is here to stay!

INFORMATION PROVIDER FOR THE PRIVATE INVESTOR

No matter how familiar an investor may be with dealing in options, one thing is certain: to maximise profits in the volatile traded options market requires access to the most accurate and up-to-date information available.

Until recently the private investor has been at a distinct disadvantage in this respect with this type of information being the exclusive property of the privileged elite able to afford the required leased line fees.

Big Bang, however, and the introduction of The Stock Exchange's new SEAQ (Stock Exchange Automated Quotations) system resolved this anomaly, and this has meant that Prestel CitiService* can now bring you more accurate traded option prices faster than ever before – and at a price affordable to the private investor.

Launched as a joint venture between BT and ICV Information Systems Ltd in 1984, CitiService now has over 15,000 users nationwide and is already helping thousands of private investors, company executives and professional advisers to make better informed and more profitable decisions every day.

Two traded option services available are as follows:

1. CitiService SEAQ: A real time prices service.
2. Fund Manager: An automatic daily update facility allowing further analysis to be undertaken off-line.

CitiService SEAQ

This service provides up-to-the-minute market prices direct from the market makers covering all traded options.

Calls and puts are provided with the bid, ask and last traded price plus the last trade for each strike price (Fig. A1.1) – information that is especially essential in a market where price volatility can lead, at a moment's notice, to violent price fluctuations. In addition, option volumes are quoted for the previous day's trading (Fig. A1.2).

As well as the very latest prices, you can also receive vital news and company

*Prestel CitiService, Woodsted House, 72 Chertsey Road, Woking, Surrey.

```
ICV 04862 27431              781907a           0p
            Calls Puts              Calls  Puts
Ald Lyon      0    0  Br. Aero       45     9
Amstrad     154  144  Br. Airw      200    25
BAA         258  105  Br. Cmwth       1     0
BAT          12    4  Br. Gas         6   702
BTR           4   40  Br. Pet       763  1380
Barclays      5    5  Br. Tel        52    17
Bass          2    0  Britoil       152   550
Beecham     390   55  Cable & W       1     4
Blue Cir    153   29  Cadbury         0     0
Boots       457  189  CommUnion     107   125

Total option market volumes:

Calls   14,228      Puts    6,153

7 Back 9 Forward 0 Index
```

FIG. A1.1 SE option volumes: 19 February 1988.

```
                                  22FEB88 11:25
   Br. Gas p/pd              call option for Apr

      Bid    Ask    High    Low    P.Clse
   130-00  131-00  132-00  130-08  130-08

Stk    Bid    Ask    Trade   TimeOLT
120    13-00  15-00  14-00   10:15
130     7-00   9-00   8-00   10:50
140     3-00   4-08
160     0-12   1-08
180     CAB    1-00
200     CAB    1-00

Calls:    —      2 Jul   3 Oct 4    —
Puts:    5 Apr   6 Jul   7 Oct 8    —
F FT-SE 100      T Top 10      Q Quotes
 *0# Exit        O Options     H Help
```

FIG. A1.2 British Gas: call options for April.

announcements immediately plus recommendations from leading brokers the moment they are issued.

Subscription to CitiService SEAQ for a non-professional user is £42 + VAT per quarter with an on-line time charge of 30p per minute. Access can be made either using an adapted TV set, personal computer or a dedicated terminal. Telephone calls are charged at a local call rate.

Fund Manager

To meet the growing needs of option investors wishing to analyse market trends, CitiService now offers an automatic traded option price feed capable of linking into an array of technical analysis software.

This feed delivers the closing mid, high and low prices, plus volume figures on the underlying share prices, automatically to your personal computer and will benefit anybody wishing to perform technical investment analysis using regularly updated data.

The service links directly into the Synergy 'OptionMaster Plus', Rochester Computer Systems' 'Chart Analyst 2', and Rowan Investments' 'Indexia' software packages, or can equally well be incorporated into other programs.

Subscription to the Fund Manager traded options feed is £150 per quarter or £450 per year. If accessed after 6.00 p.m., no time charges apply and the telephone charge is at a local call and off-peak rate.

Both these services require registration on Prestel (£6.50 per quarter for a residential user) and this can be arranged, together with equipment if necessary, by CitiService.

APPENDIX TWO

EQUITY OPTIONS CALENDAR

TABLE A2.1 Equity options calendar.

Series	Start dealing	Last day dealing	Last day assignment
1988	1987/8	1988	1988
Aug 88	Nov 19	Aug 10	Aug 11
Sep 88	Dec 17	Sep 28	Sep 29
Oct 88	Jan 21	Oct 26	Oct 27
Nov 88	Feb 18	Nov 23	Nov 24
Dec 88	Mar 17	Dec 21	Dec 22
1989	1988	1989	1989
Jan 89	Apr 21	Jan 25	Jan 26
Feb 89	May 19	Feb 22	Feb 23
Mar 89	Jun 16	Mar 29	Mar 30
Apr 89	Jul 28	Apr 12	Apr 13
May 89	Aug 11	May 17	May 18

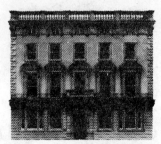

SPECIALIST TRADED OPTIONS
STOCKBROKER

After extensive research on behalf of
the private investor Richard Hexton
can recommend the services of:-

Allied Provincial Limited

Member of the Securities Association
and the International Stock Exchange.
25-27 Mosley Street, Newcastle upon Tyne, NE1 1YF.
Telephone 091 261 9957

Allied Provincial Ltd. have various branches across
the country. The Newcastle upon Tyne branch has a
department specialising only in:-

TRADED OPTIONS

In view of the gearing and volatile nature of Traded
Options where significant profits can be made in
extremely short periods, Richard Hexton realises that
you, as a private investor, might welcome specialist help
and advice from a Stockbroker.

Richard Hexton can therefore recommend
Bob Foster-Moore who specialises in Traded Options for
the private investor at Allied Provincial Ltd.

He will be more than willing to discuss such areas as:-

- Market/Stock direction
- Opening/Closing positions
- Various Option strategies

If you require further details please
send the coupon to Allied Provincial Ltd.
Alternatively you may prefer to discuss
your own personal requirements with
Bob Foster-Moore at Allied Provincial Ltd.
in which case I would suggest you phone
him on 091 261 9957.

Richard Hexton

INFORMATION REQUEST FORM Please send me full details of your client services.
Please send this completed form to: Allied Provincial Ltd., 25-27 Mosley Street, Newcastle upon Tyne NE1 1YF.

Mr/Mrs/Ms (Please delete as appropriate)   TITLE _____

CHRISTIAN NAMES _____ SURNAME _____

ADDRESS _____

_____ POST CODE _____

TELEPHONE No. (OFFICE) _____ (HOME) _____

WARNING
Options are very volatile.
You should only invest amounts
that you can afford to lose.

EXAMPLE CONTRACT NOTES

CONTRACT NOTE

We have [BOUGHT] for

Account Number [GOTTL0002] ACTING AS AGENTS

TRADED OPTION

Bargain Date & Tax Point   29 DEC 1987   for settlement [CASH]
Reference

SECURITY 8443135

	5 JAGUAR	43p	£2,150.00
EX TIME 00:00	CALL OPTIONS/APT/300P		

COMMISSION	£53.75	
V A T @ 15%	£9.03	
OTHER EXPENSES	£6.50	
		£69.28

ESQ.,

TOTAL   £2,219.28

For the purposes of Value Added Tax and Capital Gains Tax it is recommended that this Note be retained.

Subject to the rules, customs, usages and interpretations of The Stock Exchange and/or the Exchange on which the transaction was effected.

Members of the Stock Exchange
A member of the △ ■ ■ Group of Companies

FIG. A3.1 Contract note I.

APPENDIX 3

Bought By order of:			002	Our Ref MCB024	Bgn Date/VAT Point 16 June 86
Richard Duncan Hexton Esq, Traded Option Account					
Opening					HEX34458
A L D O C T 330*Option Contracts each for the call of 1000 Allied-Lyons Plc Ord 25p to expire 6pm 22/10/86					

AMOUNT	PRICE	CONSIDERATION
2	£0.37	740.00 N
8-62540-5	2 Contracts at £1.50	3.00 T
	Transfer Stamp	0 N
	Commission	18.50 T
	2.5% on £740.00	
	VAT 15.00%	3.22
FOR SETTLEMENT CASH TOTAL = £		764.72

VAT SUB TOTALS	TAXABLE ITEMS EXCLUDING VAT 21.50	EXEMPT ITEMS 0	E. & O.E.

V.A.T. Symbols; T = Taxable; E = Exempt; N = Outside the Scope.

FIG. A3.2 Contract note II.

Sold By order of:		002	Our Ref NDS006	Bgn Date/VAT Point 1 July 86

Richard Duncan Hexton Esq, Traded Option Account

Closing   HEX34458

A L D   O C T 330 * Option Contracts each for the call of 1000
Allied-Lyons Plc Ord 25p to expire 6pm 22/10/86

AMOUNT	PRICE	CONSIDERATION
2	£0.50	1000.00 N

	2 Contracts at £1.50	3.00 T
	Transfer Stamp	0 N
8-62540-5	Duplicate contract	
	Commission	12.50 T
	1.25% on £1000.00	
	VAT 15.00%	2.32

FOR SETTLEMENT   CASH   TOTAL = £   982.18

VAT SUB TOTALS	TAXABLE ITEMS EXCLUDING VAT 15.50	EXEMPT ITEMS 0	E. & O.E.

V.A.T. Symbols; T = Taxable; E = Exempt; N = Outside the Scope.

FIG. A3.3 Contract note III.

GLOSSARY

Abandon (to) To allow an option to expire without exercising it.

Assignment notice Formal notification from the London Options Clearing House to a writer requiring him to fulfil his contractual obligation to buy or sell the underlying security.

At-the-money option A call option or put option whose exercise price is the same as the current market price of the underlying security.

Bear market A stock market in which share prices are on a falling trend.

Black–Scholes formula A mathematical model which attempts to determine the theoretical true value of a call option.

Board offical A member of The Stock Exchange staff appointed to be responsible for the custody and execution of public limit orders and for ensuring the orderly conduct of trading in a particular options class.

Bull market A stock market in which share prices are on a rising trend.

Cabinet (CAB) Until the expiry date the price of an option is 'locked away' in 'cabinet' and the premium is worthless, unless there is a sudden movement of the stock price, in which case the premium will move out of cabinet and be worth something.

Call option A call option confers the right to buy a fixed number of shares at a specified price within a predetermined period of time.

Class of option All options of the same type pertaining to the same underlying security. Calls and puts form separate classes.

Clearing agent A clearing member of LOCH authorised by the Council of the Stock Exchange to clear business in traded options on its own behalf and for other member firms.

Clearing member A member firm which is a member of LOCH and so authorised to settle business in traded options.

Closing purchase A transaction by which a writer buys an option on exactly the same terms as an option which he has previously sold, thus terminating his liability.

Closing sale A transaction in which the holder of an option disposes of the option.

Contract The dealing unit in which traded options are bought and sold. A contract normally represents options on 1,000 shares of the underlying security.

Cover In relation to the traded options market, the underlying stock.

Crowd The market-makers and brokers' dealers at a particular trading pitch.

Equities The ordinary shares of a company.

Equity options Options of UK equity stocks dealt in the traded options market.

Exercise A formal notification to LOCH that the holder of an option wishes to exercise it by buying or selling the underlying stock.

Exercise price The price per share at which the buyer of a call option may buy, or the buyer of a put option may sell, the underlying security.

Expiry date The last day on which the holder of an option can exercise his right to purchase or sell the underlying security.

FT-SE 100 Index The Financial Times–Stock Exchange Index. It consists of 100 of the leading stock market securities ranked in terms of capitalisation.

Futures Contracts for the delivery or receipt of a certain given quantity of a deliverable asset at a specified future date.

Gearing The term used to describe the proportion between a company's fixed interest loan and preference capital and its equity. In the traded options market, it is often used when purchasing 'out-of-the-money' options, which have higher risk, but a much higher possible return on the capital invested – 'high gearing' options. Called 'leverage' in the United States.

Gilts Government and guaranteed securities on which there is no risk of default.

Index options Options on the indices of world markets.

In-the-money option A call option which has an exercise price below the current market price of the underlying security, or a put option which has an exercise price above the current market price of the underlying security.

Intrinsic value The difference between the exercise price and the price of the underlying security: a call option has intrinsic value if the exercise price of the option is lower than the underlying price of the security; a put option has intrinsic value if the exercise price of the option is higher than the price of the underlying security.

Margin The sum required as collateral from writers of London traded options.

Market-makers A member firm which, under the rules of The Stock Exchange, is permitted to make a market, as principal, in traded options.

Opening purchase A transaction in which the buyer becomes the holder of an option.

Opening sale A transaction in which the seller assumes liability for the performance of an option contract, thereby becoming the writer of that contract.

Open interest The number of traded option contracts outstanding at any time, either in a particular class or in all classes.

Out-of-the-money option A call option which has an exercise price above the current price of the underlying security, or a put option which has an exercise price below the current price of the underlying security.

PE ratios Price earnings ratios. The relationship between the price of a share and the company's net earnings attributable to that share, the result being expressed as the current share price divided by the latest available figure of earnings per share.

Premium The price of an option agreed upon by the buyer and seller. It is paid by the buyer to the seller.

Public limit board (PLB) A facility whereby clients can bid or offer options at their own price, irrespective of the current premiums quoted.

Public order member (POM) A broking firm which, being neither a market-maker nor a clearing member, deals in traded options on its own behalf, as principal, or on behalf of its clients, as agent. A POM may only deal in traded options if it has appointed a clearing agent to act on its behalf.

Put option A put option confers the right to sell a fixed number of shares at a specified price within a predetermined priod of time.

Rate of change indicator (ROC) Measure of momentum (0–100) in that it tells the investor when a move in a share price is accelerating or slowing down. (Zero to 25 is considered to be 'oversold' 75–100 is considered to be 'overbought'.)

Relative strength index (RSI) Developed by J. Welles Wilder Jr, this provides the necessary smoothing of a momentum line and also provides a constant band for smoothing purposes.

Running naked Writing/selling options without owning the underlying security. This term is often used when one side of a spread strategy has been closed, leaving the remaining written option open to run by itself.

Scrip issues The issue of shares, free of charge, by a company to its shareholders in proportion to their existing holdings.

Series All options of the same class with the same exercise price and expiry date.

Sole trader A one-director corporate member firm or an individual authorised to transact business only in the traded options market. Such a person is permitted to deal only as a market-maker or a floor agent.

Spread The purchase and sale of different series of options in the same class by the same principal.

Spread margin The margin required for an open uncovered sale which is offset by an opening purchase of contracts of a different series in the same class by the same principal.

Stochastic process/indicators Invented by George Lane, these are based on the observation that as prices increase closing prices tend to be closer to the upper end of the range. Conversely, in down trends the closing price tends to be near the lower end of the range.

Striking price See 'Exercise price'.

TALISMAN Transfer accounting, lodgement for investors, stock management for jobbers. The Stock Exchange's centralised computer settlement system for equities, set up in 1979.

Time value That part of the option premium which reflects the remaining life of an option. The longer the time remaining before expiry, the higher the time value will tend to be.

Traded option An option which can be bought and sold on the trading floor of The Stock Exchange.

Underlying security The share to which the option relates.

Unit of trading See 'Contract'.

Writer A person who executes an opening sale of an option contract.

FURTHER READING

Richard Hexton's Options Monitor, weekly traded options newsletter available from the London School of Investment, 125 Gloucester Road, London SW7 4TE Tel: 01-370 0867.

Technical Analysis Course, the London School of Investment, 125 Gloucester Road, London SW7 4TE Tel: 01-370 0867.

INDEX